T0285290

JACK THORNE

Jack Thorne's plays for the stage include *The Motive and the Cue*
(National Theatre, London, 2023); an adaptation of Hirokazu
Kore-eda's film *After Life* (National Theatre, London, 2021);
Harry Potter and the Cursed Child (Palace Theatre, London,
since 2016, and Lyric Theatre, New York, since 2018; winner of
the 2017 Olivier Award for Best New Play and the 2018 Tony
Award for Best Play); a reimagining of *A Christmas Carol* by
Charles Dickens (Old Vic Theatre, 2017, 2018, 2019); *the end of
history...* (Royal Court Theatre, 2019); a musical adaptation of
King Kong (Broadway Theatre, New York, 2018); a new version
of Georg Büchner's *Woyzeck* (Old Vic Theatre, 2017); *Junkyard*
(Headlong/Bristol Old Vic/Rose Theatre Kingston/Theatr Clwyd,
2017); *The Solid Life of Sugar Water* (Graeae Theatre Company);
Hope (Royal Court Theatre, London, 2014); adaptations of *Let the
Right One In* (National Theatre of Scotland at Dundee Rep, the
Royal Court and the Apollo Theatre, London, 2013/14) and
Stuart: A Life Backwards (Underbelly, Edinburgh, and tour, 2013);
Mydidae (Soho, 2012; Trafalgar Studios, 2013); an adaptation of
Friedrich Dürrenmatt's *The Physicists* (Donmar Warehouse,
2012); *Bunny* (Underbelly, Edinburgh, 2010; Soho, 2011); *2nd
May 1997* (Bush, 2009); *Burying Your Brother in the Pavement*
(National Theatre Connections, 2008); *When You Cure Me* (Bush,
2005; Radio 3's Drama on Three, 2006); *Fanny and Faggot*
(Pleasance, Edinburgh, 2004 and 2007; Finborough, 2007;
English Theatre of Bruges, 2007; Trafalgar Studios, 2007); and
Stacy (Tron, 2006; Arcola, 2007; Trafalgar Studios, 2007).

His radio plays include *Left at the Angel* (Radio 4, 2007), an
adaptation of *The Hunchback of Notre Dame* (2009), and an
original play *People Snogging in Public Places* (Radio 3's Wire
slot, 2009).

For television, Jack has five BAFTAs for his work on *National
Treasure* (Best Mini-Series, 2017); *This is England '90* (Best
Mini-Series, 2016); *Don't Take My Baby* (Best Single Drama,
2016); *The Fades* (Best Drama Series, 2012); *This is England '88*
(Best Mini-Series, 2012). He is also the recipient of an International
Emmy Award for *Help* (Best TV Movie/Mini-Series).

His other writing for television includes *Then Barbara Met Alan*, the BBC adaptation of Philip Pullman's *His Dark Materials*, *CripTales*, *The Eddy*, *The Accident*, *The Virtues*, *Kiri*, *Electric Dreams*, *The Last Panthers*, *Glue*, *Shameless*, *Skins* and *Cast-Offs*.

In 2022 Jack was the recipient of both the Writers' Guild of Great Britain award for Outstanding Contribution to Writing, and the Royal Television Society's award for Outstanding Contribution to British Television, and in 2023 the National Film and Television School awarded Jack their honorary fellowship.

His work for film includes the features *Enola Holmes 1* and *2*, *The Secret Garden*, *Radioactive*, *Dirt Music*, *Wonder*, *War Book*, *A Long Way Down* and *The Scouting Book for Boys*.

Jack is a patron of Graeae Theatre Company, an associate artist of The Old Vic, and a fellow of the Royal Society of Literature. He is a founding member of the pressure group Underlying Health Condition.

Jack Thorne

WHEN WINSTON WENT TO WAR WITH THE WIRELESS

A True Story About Truth

NICK HERN BOOKS
London
www.nickhernbooks.co.uk

A Nick Hern Book

When Winston Went To War With The Wireless first published as a paperback
original in Great Britain in 2023 by Nick Hern Books Limited, The Glasshouse,
49a Goldhawk Road, London W12 8QP

When Winston Went To War With The Wireless copyright © 2023 Jack Thorne

Jack Thorne has asserted his right to be identified as the author of this work

'Don't Be Cruel to a Vegetable' words and music by Leslie Sarony © 1928,
reproduced by permission of Francis Day and Hunter Ltd, London W1F 9LD

BBC copyright content reproduced courtesy of the British Broadcasting
Corporation. All rights reserved.

Cover image: photography by Johan Persson; artwork by AKA

Designed and typeset by Nick Hern Books, London
Printed in Great Britain by Mimeo Ltd, Huntingdon, Cambridgeshire PE29 6XX

A CIP catalogue record for this book is available from the British Library

ISBN   978 1 83904 222 5

CAUTION   All rights whatsoever in this play are strictly reserved. Requests
to reproduce the text in whole or in part should be addressed to the publisher.

Amateur Performing Rights   Applications for performance, including
readings and excerpts, by amateurs in the English language throughout the
world should be addressed to the Performing Rights Manager, Nick Hern
Books, The Glasshouse, 49a Goldhawk Road, London W12 8QP,
tel +44 (0)20 8749 4953, *email* rights@nickhernbooks.co.uk, except as follows:

Australia: ORiGiN Theatrical, Level 1, 213 Clarence Street, Sydney
NSW 2000, *tel* +61 (2) 8514 5201, *email* enquiries@originmusic.com.au,
web www.origintheatrical.com.au

New Zealand: Play Bureau, 20 Rua Street, Mangapapa, Gisborne, 4010,
tel +64 21 258 3998, *email* info@playbureau.com

USA and Canada: Casarotto Ramsay and Associates Ltd, see details below

Professional Performing Rights   Applications for performance by
professionals in any medium and in any language throughout the world
(including by stock companies in the USA and Canada) should be addressed to
Casarotto Ramsay and Associates Ltd, *email* rights@casarotto.co.uk,
www.casarotto.co.uk

No performance of any kind may be given unless a licence has been obtained.
Applications should be made before rehearsals begin. Publication of this play
does not necessarily indicate its availability for amateur performance.

www.nickhernbooks.co.uk/environmental-policy

When Winston Went To War With The Wireless was first
performed on 13 June 2023 (previews from 2 June) at the
Donmar Warehouse, London, with the following cast:

ISABEL SHIELDS	Kitty Archer
JOHN REITH	Stephen Campbell Moore
ARCHBISHOP OF CANTERBURY/ J. C. C. DAVIDSON	Ravin J Ganatra
STANLEY BALDWIN	Haydn Gwynne
MURIEL REITH	Mariam Haque
ERNEST BEVIN	Kevin McMonagle
CHARLIE BOWSER/ENGINEER	Luke Newberry
MUSICIAN/SPEAKER OF THE HOUSE	Seb Philpott
ARTHUR PUGH/MUSICIAN	Elliott Rennie
CLEMMIE CHURCHILL/ AMELIA JOHNSON	Laura Rogers
PETER ECKERSLEY	Shubham Saraf
WINSTON CHURCHILL	Adrian Scarborough

All other parts played by the company

Director	Katy Rudd
Designer	Laura Hopkins
Sound Designers	Ben and Max Ringham
Lighting Designer	Howard Hudson
Movement Director	Scott Graham
Composer	Gary Yershon
Video Designer and Animator	Andrzej Goulding
Casting Director	Anna Cooper CDG
Foley Consultant	Tom Espiner
Production Manager	Jim Leaver
Costume Supervisor	Lisa Aitken
Props Supervisor	Lizzie Frankl for Propworks

Associate Props Supervisor	Rachel Middlemore for Propworks
Associate Sound Designer	Ellie Isherwood
Wigs, Hair and Make-Up Supervisor	Sharon Pearson
Wigs, Hair and Make-Up Manager	Keisha Banya
Voice Coach	Charlie Hughes D'Aeth
Dialect Coach	Penny Dyer
Resident Assistant Director	Adam Karim
Assistant Set and Costume Designer	Jingyi
Assistant Sound Designer	Raffaela Pancucci
Sound Operator	Jake Hanks
Company Stage Manager	Robert Perkins
Deputy Stage Manager	Maria Gibbons
Assistant Stage Manager	Devon James-Bowen

Acknowledgements

Katy Rudd
Michael Longhurst
Laura Hopkins
Ben & Max Ringham
Craig Gilbert
Nick Morrison
Matthew Warchus
Andrew Marr
David Hendy
Georgina Born
Kate Varah
Robert Seatter
Jean Seaton
Rachel Taylor
Helena Clark
Hannah Spinks
Tom Hercock
Paul Sarony
Peter Sarony
The Estate of Alfred Noyes
The Estate of Asa Briggs
Cicely Hadman
Stuart Tubby
Mariella Johnson

J.T.

For Rachel Holroyd.
With gratitude.

'[The BBC was a] democracy of young pioneers, doomed like all the pioneering of youth to come up against the rigidity of age, discipline and experience.'

Cecil Lewis, 'Broadcasting from Within'

Characters

JOHN REITH, *thirty-seven, conflicted, confident, with a scar on his left cheek*

WINSTON CHURCHILL, *fifty-two, balding, barrel-chested, bellicose*

ISABEL SHIELDS, *late twenties, perfectly spoken, rather ornate*

PETER ECKERSLEY, *thirty-four, chief engineer. Pipe in his mouth, slouches about*

STANLEY BALDWIN, *fifty-eight, Prime Minister of the country, cleverer than he first appears*

J. C. C. DAVIDSON, *thirty-seven, deputy chief civil commissioner, deviously devoted*

ERNEST BEVIN, *forty-five, leader of the Transport and General Workers' Union, wears the weight*

ARTHUR PUGH, *fifty-six, Chair of the TUC's Special Industrial Committee, brow-beaten, overwrought*

AMELIA JOHNSON, *forties, newsreader, ramrod straight*

CHARLIE BOWSER, *early twenties, beautiful, inside and out, a ghost of a past*

CLEMENTINE CHURCHILL, *forty-one, witty, caring and frequently merciless*

MURIEL REITH, *thirties, full of a get-up-and-go that's frequently thwarted*

JIX, *sixty, Home Secretary, quite a traditional home secretary*

THE ARCHBISHOP OF CANTERBURY, *seventy-eight, patrician, stooped*

All other parts (and there are quite a few, see below) should be played by members of the company.

UNION MEN
HELGA, *a singer*
ENGINEER
H. G. WELLS
HELENA MILLAIS
BEATRICE LILLIE
A screaming MAN
ELLA FITZPATRICK
SANDY POWELL
A coughing WOMAN
COMMANDER KENWORTHY
DUKE OF CORNWALL
GERRY, *a Foley artist*
BILLY BENNETT
SPEAKER OF THE HOUSE
LLOYD GEORGE
MORGAN JONES
BRUCE, *a spoons player*
MARION CRAN

And FOLEY ARTISTS – *I suggest some of the Foley in the script. I hope there'll be room for a lot more in an actual production.*

Note

News bulletins in the play have been adapted from BBC bulletins between 1 May and 13 May 1926.

This text went to press before the end of rehearsals and so may differ slightly from the play as performed.

Prologue

There's darkness. Pure darkness.

Then emerging from the darkness come UNION MEN, *their faces dark, their headlamps filling the stage and their song filling the theatre.*

UNION MEN.
> When the union's inspiration through the workers' blood
>> shall run,
> There can be no power greater anywhere beneath the sun;
> Yet what force on earth is weaker than the feeble strength
>> of one,
> But the union makes us strong.

> Solidarity forever,
> Solidarity forever,
> Solidarity forever,
> For the union makes us strong.

And they are gone.

ACT ONE

Scene One

HELGA *is a singer, unaccustomed to radio, the* ENGINEER *is seemingly in control.*

ENGINEER. Just give it your best, nice and slow is what I'd recommend.

HELGA. One can hardly slow down the music. The tempo is –

ENGINEER. Otherwise we get complaints, dear. People like to hear the words, you see…

HELGA. I don't see how…

ENGINEER. The trouble being, of course, they lack the equipment. Only a very expensive receiver can do justice to transmission and only then when signals are very strong. Mostly all they hear is the equivalent to someone screaming in their privy.

HELGA. Probably better if I don't think about screaming in the privy…

ENGINEER. Those are not my words, they're the words of Peter Eckersley, my boss. Great man. So slow the tempo and avoid… well, final advice, avoid nipping about too much if you can help it.

HELGA. Nipping about?

ENGINEER. High, low and then high again, it distorts it. Which, if you're in an over-large and poorly insulated privy, well…

HELGA. You want me to *not* sing the high notes?

ENGINEER. Oh, you need to sing them, dear, but make them a *tad* lower. If you can.

HELGA. Make the high notes lower?

ENGINEER. Yes. (*Picking up a receiver.*) Hello, control room, this is transmission studio number three, signal me when you're ready for testing please.

HELGA. You do understand, I have to sing the notes as they are laid out at the tempo they're laid out in.

A light comes on. He watches it closely.

ENGINEER. One, two, three, four, five, six, seven, eight, nine, ten. When Mary had a *little* scran, she often felt quite hungry, so everywhere she ever went she took an extra sandwich with her…

The light goes off.

Watch for the light to turn on again, when it does – sing.

JOHN REITH *enters, on the storm.*

HELGA. Who is this?

ENGINEER. Are you commandeering, sir?

PETER ECKERSLEY *rushes in after him.*

PETER. I've scrambled everyone to look for you.

REITH. Studio three felt the best.

ENGINEER. It's happened?

REITH. It's happened and we're about to broadcast it.

PETER. I can't believe they've done it.

HELGA. Done what?

REITH. The TUC's finally fired the gun…

PETER. Or the Government have…

HELGA. Strike? A General Strike?

ENGINEER. They're all going out?

PETER. *Daily Mail* printers refused to set an editorial condemning the TUC, Government called off negotiations,

the TUC had no choice... Everyone – every union – is
striking.

REITH (*over* PETER*'s lines*). Miss Shields! Isabel!

    AMELIA JOHNSON *enters from off in a cocktail dress.*

AMELIA. I'm ready. I'm ready.

PETER. We'll need five minutes.

REITH. Two minutes.

AMELIA. Oh. Where's my –

REITH. I can handle this.

    ISABEL SHIELDS *enters after.*

HELGA. I need to call my mother.

ISABEL. I've got a statement from them and a rather shorter
one from Downing Street.

AMELIA. I just can't find my jacket. Do I need a jacket?

ISABEL (*to* AMELIA). With shoulders like that? I'd have
thought so.

REITH. This is my responsibility.

PETER. What does that mean?

REITH. I'll take lead. I'll do it.

AMELIA. But isn't it my –

REITH. Peter – cue me in –

AMELIA. But don't I do the news? I do the news.

HELGA. Can I leave? Can I get to a phone?

ENGINEER *and* PETER. No.

REITH. Hold out your hands.

    AMELIA *does, they're shaking.* REITH *holds his out,*
    they're still.

    I have this.

PETER (*over the receiver*). This is studio three, we will be taking over the airwaves as part of an emergency transmission –

REITH *sits and begins to make notes.*

ENGINEER. We're scheduled anyway.

PETER. Then have studio two scheduled to go after we're done.

ENGINEER. Yes, sir.

ISABEL *gently places the statements in front of REITH.*

ISABEL. This is everything we have, sir.

PETER. You know what you're going to say?

REITH. No. Count me in.

He settles himself, he scans the pages, he looks up, PETER *signals – they're live.*

This is London and all stations calling.

Negotiations between the Government and trade unions have broken down. The Trade Unions Congress have today declared a General Strike. The strike will commence at midnight tonight. According to an official memorandum of the Trades Union Congress the following trades are involved in the strike call: all transport, printing trades, iron and steel, electric and gas workers, and all those in building work. Sanitary services are to be continued however and there will be no interference with healthcare.

WINSTON CHURCHILL *enters, humming, he pours himself a whisky* – FOLEY ARTISTS *pour water from one glass into another glass – he goes over to an ice bucket – they put two pebbles in the glass – he sits in his chair.*

The Government have declared a state of national emergency exists and that as a precautionary measure they've moved detachments of troops and military vehicles into designated zones throughout the country for, and I quote, 'the maintenance of law and order and the protection of life and property'.

May we appeal to all our listeners to make this strike as short and as painless as possible and to preserve goodwill so as to find a way out of this deadlock.

The BBC have received a message from the Prime Minister, it reads as follows: 'Be steady. Remember that peace on earth comes from men of good will.' I will repeat this. 'Be steady. Remember that peace on earth comes from men of good will.'

Beat.

'Be steady. Remember that peace on earth comes from men of good will.'

This is London. More when we have it.

He stands up. He signals to the ENGINEER *who passes it to another studio.*

There. There.

He breathes out.

Did I repeat the statement three times?

PETER. Yes, sir.

REITH. Was that a mistake?

PETER. No. They won't be able to dock our coverage now, you know –

REITH. Did I really read it out three times?

PETER. You did.

REITH. Well. Good. Good. Get her ready for the air.

He indicates HELGA.

It's done. They did it.

PETER. They did.

REITH *rubs his face. He looks at* HELGA.

REITH. Do you know 'Abide with Me'?

HELGA. No.

REITH. Then sing what you can. This country will need all the
distractions it can find at the moment.

Lights click out. Only CHURCHILL *is left.*

CHURCHILL (*sings*).
Then raise the scarlet standard high,
Beneath its shade we'll live and die,
Though cowards flinch and traitors sneer,
We'll keep the red flag flying here.

He raises a glass. The lights turn off completely.

Scene Two

ISABEL. A typical day at the BBC.
Well, it was very exciting.
Mostly exciting.
We'd have allsorts trooping in.
The London Radio Dance Band –

There's a dash of Dance Band.

The Daventry Quartet –

There's a dash of strings.

There were plays like –
Light and Shade, a comedy by L. du Garde Peach.

FRANCIS. I would love to talk, darling, but sadly I've my foot
trapped in a bucket.

A FOLEY ARTIST *drops a bucket on the floor. There's the
sound of laughter.*

ISABEL. And wonderful celebrities like Sir Oliver Lodge
talking on worlds and atoms, Doctor C. W. Saleeby on
health. Though the less said about H. G. Wells the better. The
man squeaked. He squeaked.

H. G. WELLS (*squeaky*). Face the world. Learn its ways, watch it, be careful of too-hasty guesses at its meaning. In the end you will find clues to it all.

ISABEL. In the end you'll find your voice is poorly suited to radio, Mr Squeaky Wells. Peter Eckersley, our wonderful chief engineer.

PETER *wanders onto stage*.

Even manufactured a special room, just for H. G. Wells, but did he squeak?

H. G. WELLS (*squeak*). Yes.

ISABEL. Of course he did.

And finally my favourite thing on the schedule – the comedians – everyone from the mysterious A. J. Alan to Joe Murgatroyd and his tiffs with his wife Blossom, to Miss Helena Millais with her *Light Songs and Fragments from Life*.

HELENA MILLAIS. Ullo, me ducks, 'ere I am again with me old string bag and nothing to sing bar 'Ours Is a Nice 'Ouse Ours Is'.

ISABEL. There were only two rules:

PETER. 'If you sneeze you will deafen millions.'

ISABEL. And –

PETER. 'No gags on Scotsmen, Welshmen, clergymen, drink or medical matters.'

ISABEL. Open house on the Irish of course.

The news was never really central to our template. The BBC had been prevented from presenting the news until seven p.m. at night. Newspapers worried it would interfere with circulation if people could get the news for free.

But the General Strike meant everything changed. For newspapers could not be printed or distributed and that meant – well, that meant the wireless had power, you see? It was the only information source for many as to what was actually happening.

And so much was happening. Arguments raged in
Parliament, and all across the country...

Yes. The General Strike changed everything – and the BBC
– it turned out – was right in the centre of it –

Scene Three

CHURCHILL *walks through the clock corridor in the Palace of
Westminster.* ERNEST BEVIN *pursues him across the floor.*
ARTHUR PUGH *just behind.* FOLEY ARTISTS *provide
echoey steps.*

BEVIN. Mr Churchill. Chancellor. Mr Churchill. Ernest Bevin
and Arthur Pugh – here to talk to you and to the Prime
Minister. Ready to resume negotiations. We've shown our
hand, you've shown yours. Time to talk more, don't you think?

CHURCHILL. Ernest, you say?

BEVIN. You know who I am, sir, and as General Secretary of
the Transport and General Workers' Union –

CHURCHILL. More than shown your hand, young Ernest,
you've gone and taken your bloody clothes off.

BEVIN. It was purely *your* unwillingness to resume talks that
left us –

CHURCHILL. I respect you enormously – Ernest, but the time
for negotiation has passed. You weren't able to control your
people – the *Daily Mail* printers –

PUGH. The printers attacked without TUC support –

CHURCHILL. – would not publish and that rather forced us
into our position, you see –

PUGH. The *Daily Mail* was calling us revolutionaries.
Besmirching our patriotism.

CHURCHILL. The freedom of the press is the freedom to occasionally get things wrong.

BEVIN. Sir, let us sit down again. Find a new way through.

CHURCHILL. It is your strike. Ernest. That means it's yours to call off. We will sit and talk again when you do. Until then, the Prime Minister – and myself have a country in chaos to govern. Good day to you.

He makes to walk on.

BEVIN. A high-stakes game. All of this.

CHURCHILL. Interesting that you are the one to bring the word 'game' into it.

BEVIN. You haven't understood the problem. You haven't seen how badly our miners are being treated.

CHURCHILL. And you haven't seen the balance sheets of our country's economy that I daily struggle with.

BEVIN. The mine owners are taking too much. They're destroying the industry.

CHURCHILL. The mine owners own the mines.

BEVIN. Then if you'd just kept the subsidy a little longer, we might have been able to resolve…

CHURCHILL. This country has a war debt. To get it back on its feet again will take careful fiscal rectitude –

BEVIN (*rage rising*). But you couldn't provide that subsidy, could you, Chancellor? Because you'd crashed our economy by returning us to the God-awful Gold Standard…

There's a silence, he seems to have hit a nerve.

CHURCHILL. A match?

A FOLEY ARTIST *strikes a piece of wood against some sandpaper. Another puts his lips around a piece of circular leather.* CHURCHILL *coughs lightly. He inhales deeply.*

Working men, you always have matches. Lucifers. Fire.
Whereas men at my station always have to ask for – it.
I serve my castle, Mr Bevin, you serve yours. You think I am
dangerous for your castle, and I think you are dangerous to
mine. You fired the bullet, and we – the Government – are
trying our best to deflect it. The question is whether my
castle is under more substantial attack – or whether, now,
it might be yours.

AMELIA (*through speakers*). It is the 4th May and eight a.m.
precisely, this is London and all stations calling.

CHURCHILL. Ready the hot oil. The troops are massing. The
bugle cry has been heard. You are under siege.

AMELIA. In half an hour we'll have Jack Hylton debating Sir
Landon Ronald on the respective merits of jazz and classical
music. But first, here's Beatrice Lillie with something to
amuse us –

BEATRICE LILLIE.
There's a new society
Called the RSPCV
To protect spring greens
And the garden beans
From undue cruelty.
It's a great and noble task,
And here's what the members ask:
Don't be cruel to a vegetabuel.
Always take its part.
Don't be cruel to a vegetabuel.
Don't forget a lettuce has a heart.
If you please, don't split peas,
Just because they're tasty to the tongue;
And don't forget, when you order sprouts,
You're going to rob a cabbage of its young.

In his office REITH *turns off the radio*.

PETER (*indicating the radio*). Not one of her best.

REITH *smiles and nods*.

Been waiting for you at the front desk.

REITH. Ah. Well, I never left so...

PETER. You slept here?

REITH. I've slept worse places. Tell me, Peter, are we shipshape?

PETER. The switchboards are jammed. Mostly with people wondering whether we can put out an announcement about whatever event they've had to cancel.

REITH (*laughing*). Oh my –

PETER. You can laugh, I spent fifteen minutes on the board to a woman from Worthing who was adamant we should announce the cancellation of her lawn bowls tournament. She said it was our duty. In this crisis. Because her local paper the *Worthing – Tribune* –

REITH. I doubt it's called the *Worthing Tribune*.

PETER (*they laugh together*). – is unable to print anything.

A FOLEY ARTIST *knocks on a piece of wood.*

REITH. Who?

ISABEL. Mr Reith, I've got you your numbers.

REITH. Thank you, Isabel.

ISABEL *comes into the office, full of intent.*

ISABEL. Of our employees, two hundred and forty-seven men and girls live near enough to Savoy Hill or have private transport facilities to enable them to reach work.

PETER. That's more than I thought.

ISABEL. Forty-six others will require special transport.

REITH. How many won't be able to get in at all?

ISABEL. Fifteen men and twenty-seven girls. With a bit of jiggery-pokery we can cope.

REITH. Good. Let me know when we get more from Reuters.

ISABEL *hurries out.*

PETER. We need some sort of general statement. About these notices. Stop the call jam.

REITH. Yes. Let's write something to go out before the, uh, the Shakespeare debate… 'There are – so – there are so many of these events that we do not feel justified in broadcasting messages in connection with them and' –

A knock on a piece of wood.

Who?

DAVIDSON. I hope I'm not interrupting.

REITH. Ah. Minister. You're very welcome. Peter Eckersley. Chief Engineer. The honourable J. C. C. Davidson. He's been appointed Deputy Chief Civil Commissioner for the strike. He will be looking after us.

DAVIDSON. Or you will be looking after me. How do you do?

REITH (*to* PETER). 'We would advise all listeners to make their own enquiries as best they can, as to any event in which they are interested. The BBC cannot broadcast announcements on the subject nor can we answer enquiries. Particularly not about your lawn bowls competition in Worthing.'

DAVIDSON. Ah. Worthing. I have a great-aunt in Worthing.

REITH. Get Amelia or Hilda to read it. A female voice sounds less confrontational.

DAVIDSON. Unless it's my great-aunt. Her voice sounds positively threatening.

PETER *exits with a smile.*

REITH. Tea? I can get the girl to fetch –

DAVIDSON. I'm fine.

REITH. Just writing a bulletin.

DAVIDSON. Which is why I'm here. The Government and the press have agreed to your need to broadcast more than once during the –

REITH. I want to do broadcasts at eight a.m., ten a.m., one p.m., four p.m., seven p.m. and nine-thirty p.m. That's not excessive, in the absence of the newspapers being able to print –

DAVIDSON. In that absence, as it happens, the Government will be filling the gap with a paper of our own – the *British Gazette*.

REITH. You're launching a newspaper?

DAVIDSON. Winston Churchill is editing it himself. But that doesn't make – doesn't alter the BBC's significance. I will make clear your request is to be given greatest priority.

REITH. Further to that, if I'm not allowed reporters in the field I've only one news source – Reuters –

DAVIDSON. And the admiralty.

Beat.

It perhaps would be useful… In light of your request for more bulletins. If you could just talk me through what you're likely to read –

There's a hesitation. REITH *doesn't like this.*

REITH. I'm still writing.

DAVIDSON. A rough sense.

REITH *considers, and then looks down at his paper.*

REITH. We have a report on the supply systems in place.

DAVIDSON. Good. That sounds useful.

REITH. One hundred and ninety-eight coal vessels are held up in South Wales ports.

DAVIDSON. Is it that many?

REITH. We have a report on Prince Henry's visit to the Annual Banquet of the Royal Academy.

DAVIDSON. Ahh yes, I actually attended that, remarkably good evening. Overshadowed a bit at the end. Lots of running about.

REITH. A report on the Annual Stock Exchange London-to-Brighton walk.

DAVIDSON. Who won?

REITH. A man called Ayles in eight hours fifty-one minutes and twenty-four-and-a-half seconds.

DAVIDSON. Good for him.

REITH. And Lloyd George speaking in Cambridge –

DAVIDSON. Saying?

REITH. On the coal crisis versus ideas of Bolshevism…

DAVIDSON. Specifically?

REITH. …saying the coal crisis had and has nothing to do with Bolshevism or any kind of Communism, that it was an honest trade dispute where the parties have been unable to come to an agreement.

DAVIDSON. That's perhaps less useful. Conjecture, you see.

REITH. Ah.

DAVIDSON. We don't want to confuse the general public. Perhaps we should not include that in the bulletin.

REITH. I don't see how –

DAVIDSON. And what else?

REITH. The weather.

DAVIDSON. I can't see anything contentious about that. Thank you. And good day.

He makes to exit.

REITH. Lloyd George led us for many years…

DAVIDSON. And admirably. But for now, let's focus on facts, not opinion, don't you think?

REITH. And is it the same for the Labour Party – they've requested a slot for Ramsay MacDonald to speak –

DAVIDSON. Yes, I can't see how Ramsay MacDonald will help matters either.

REITH. And yet the Prime Minister's people are already telling me he will come on –

DAVIDSON. If the Prime Minister wishes to speak on the BBC – well, he's the Prime Minister – the public should hear from their government, don't you think? Especially in times of crisis. I'll run it up the pole about your bulletins. Good day, Mr Reith.

He leaves the office.

REITH *rubs his face. He makes his way over back to the radio. He thinks a moment. He looks at the door Davidson left by, knowing he's made a big decision.*

He turns on the radio. ISABEL *sounds through it.*

ISABEL (*recorded*). The problem with sound… The delight of sound…

And then a light turns on – ISABEL *is revealed.*

Sound is secretive… Sound unleashes thoughts… For instance, my brother – he's dead now – my brother when he came back from the war – he, uh, he couldn't bear the sound of something boiling or frying – anything that involved boiling or frying he –

A MAN *stands screaming at the back of the stage.*

My mother. I was younger then – my mother could only cook when he was out of the house – because otherwise –

The MAN *screams again.*

So my father would take him to the pub before every mealtime – lunch and dinner – not sure that ultimately helped him actually – but it's what he did –

The MAN *screams again.*

Sounds takes you to places you want to go and sometimes to places you don't.

CHARLIE. John…

REITH *turns towards* CHARLIE BOWSER, *standing at the side of the stage. And then* CHARLIE *is gone.*

REITH *lies down on the floor.*

ISABEL. Did you know one of the hardest sounds for effects artists to recreate is that of a gunshot? Even if you fire the real thing it sounds like a champagne cork. Extraordinary, really – that that would be one of the sounds that would fox them so.

Sound unlocks you.

And then CHARLIE *is lying beside* REITH. *And they're smiling.*

REITH. They, looking back, all the eastern side beheld
Of Paradise, so late their happy seat,
Waved over by that flaming brand, the gate
With dreadful faces thronged and fiery arms:
Some natural tears they dropped, but wiped them soon;
The world was all before them, where to choose
Their place of rest, and Providence their guide;
They, hand in hand, with wandering steps and slow,
Through Eden took their solitary way.

Do you like it?

CHARLIE. It's sad.

REITH. I wouldn't say it was sad. It's magnificent.

CHARLIE. It's magnificently sad.

REITH. This might be Eden.

CHARLIE. And you'd want to be here?

REITH. Always. Especially with you.

CHARLIE *smiles.*

I carried two photographs in my wallet through France, one was of my father, the other was of – you.

CHARLIE. As you've told me many times, as if it proves
    something –

    REITH *looks at him, ready to argue back, but changes his
    mind.*

    And I suspect Eden should be somewhere warmer than the
    Monzie Falls.

    REITH *laughs.* CHARLIE *gets to his feet. He jumps about,
    trying to shake the cold out of himself.*

    I like it when you laugh. You don't laugh often enough.

REITH. All I meant, with the photograph is –

CHARLIE. Shall we swim?

REITH. I've nothing to wear.

CHARLIE. Neither have I. Shall we swim?

REITH. Out there I – I seem unable to consider what this world
    is. Here – everything feels more certain. Your photograph
    took me home.

CHARLIE. Then thank the Lord for dysentery.

REITH. Out there I just see –

CHARLIE. I'm trying to make you smile again, Johnnie, and
    you seem determined to –

    REITH *laughs.*

REITH. I do, don't I?

CHARLIE. All the same, I'm having a ripping day. Are you?
    Please don't say something poetic in response. A simple yes
    or no –

REITH. Yes. Yes. I am.

CHARLIE. Then let's swim. You've read, you've talked, now
    let's do. The water will be freezing, we will be destroyed, but
    we will be destroyed together.

    CHARLIE *begins to strip.*

REITH. You're wild.

CHARLIE. I'm a wildling.

He howls like a wolf.

Come on.

He howls like a wolf again.

Don't be a spoilsport.

He howls like a wolf again.

REITH *bends to untie his shoes and becomes his older self.*

REITH. I will not question you, God, I will go where you send
me. Whatever comes my way – you will provide answers.
I will read the Scripture, I will learn from it, I will – I am
a servant of you, I am a servant of God.

CHARLIE. Come on.

He approaches REITH *and starts to try and undress him.*

REITH. Take a letter –

ISABEL. Yes, sir.

REITH. Dear sir, due to the extraordinary nature of the daily
news cycle, we will be unable to accommodate the Right
Honourable Member for Leicester, Mr Ramsay MacDonald, at
this present time. But when time allows in the future we would
be honoured to have him in our studios – et cetera, et cetera.

ISABEL. Yes, sir?

CHARLIE. Johnnie. Come on.

REITH. And tell whomever's editing the bulletin to exclude any
recordings we have of Lloyd George's speech from it –

ISABEL. Yes, sir.

Scene Four

CHURCHILL *follows* JIX *down a corridor.*

CHURCHILL. Home Secretary. Jix. A moment of your time.

JIX. Can't stop, a crowd's been attempting to stop traffic going through the Blackwall Tunnel.

CHURCHILL. Is nowhere sacred?

JIX. The police were sent in. There was a baton charge. I need an allocation – from the Treasury – more money for temporary recruitment. I need special constables.

CHURCHILL. How many would you like?

JIX. Fifty thousand.

CHURCHILL. To protect the Blackwall Tunnel? With the Prime Minister's permission, you'll have them. The Treasury will prove no barrier.

JIX. I think I'll put out an appeal on the BBC.

CHURCHILL. You must. And we'll put out a piece in the *British Gazette*. We'll get your numbers.

JIX *turns to* CHURCHILL, *nods, and makes to walk on.*

You think Baldwin has this?

JIX. No time for insurrection.

CHURCHILL. You're being charged in the Blackwall Tunnel. There are temporary food distribution centres in Hyde Park. And we've warships delivering food –

JIX. Two loads already delivered. We're rendering them ineffective.

CHURCHILL. They are baying like spayed hounds in the Commons.

JIX. I know your ambition, Winston, but now is not the time.

CHURCHILL. At times of crisis the country needs strong leadership.

JIX. The Prime Minister will be strong enough.

CHURCHILL. I hope and pray you're right.

Scene Five

REITH *stands alone in his office*.

ELLA (*on radio*). This is London and this is *Women's Hour*. Today we are debating the notion 'That Woman is Nearer Barbarism than Man', that promises to be fascinating, then Lady Duff Gordon will be joining us to speak on 'fashions' and giving us advice in and out of shops, so get your notebook open for that – and we will conclude with a rather scurrilous / edition of Ariel's Society Gossip. So much to –

CHURCHILL (*speaking over*). You have the damn thing on in here too?

REITH *turns off the radio*.

REITH. Ah…

CHURCHILL. The girl let me up. I hope you don't mind. Winston. Churchill.

REITH. I know who you are, Mr Churchill. John Reith.

The two shake hands.

CHURCHILL. How on earth do you get any thinking done?

REITH. I manage well enough.

CHURCHILL. Who is she?

REITH. Miss Ella Fitzpatrick.

CHURCHILL. Melodious speaking voice. I can see why you picked her. *Woman's Hour*, did she call it? I must tell Clemmie. Do they only get an hour?

REITH. There is also *Children's Hour* and *Men's Hour*. They're rather popular.

CHURCHILL. Then that is wonderful news indeed.

Beat.

I suppose it'd be expecting too much that a drink –

REITH. Whisky?

CHURCHILL. You speak my language.

REITH *makes him a drink.*

Suffrage – that sort of thing?

REITH. Sorry?

CHURCHILL. This *Woman's Hour.* Along with barbarism. She did say they'd be discussing barbarism?

REITH. Did you come here to talk about women, Mr Churchill?

CHURCHILL. I did not. I never talk about women on a full stomach. And I've just had a fine lunch.

REITH. Then how may I help you?

CHURCHILL *takes the glass from him.*

CHURCHILL. On the contrary, I am here to help you.

REITH. Are you?

CHURCHILL. The sound of history. I offer you the sound of history being made. For your – wireless.

REITH. I do wish to be able to put a microphone in Parliament, if only to pick up on key debates, and at this time –

CHURCHILL. No. No microphone in – No. That's a – God-awful – is nowhere sacred? His Majesty's Parliament.

No, I have a wonderful idea – the *British Gazette* is being put together as we speak – a government newspaper that will change –

REITH. I've heard about your newspaper. How can I help the *Gazette*?

CHURCHILL. Why the constant emphasis on you helping me? It's like you've never been given a present before.

REITH. What are you proposing, sir?

CHURCHILL. Sounds. We can help you with sounds. Historic sounds. We go to press in three hours. Two hundred and thirty thousand copies. I think the BBC should capture it.

REITH. The noise of it going to press?

CHURCHILL. The roar of the printers. Have you ever been in a printers when it's giving out? It's quite the scream.

REITH *sits back in his chair.*

REITH. How did you persuade the other newspaper proprietors? That you – weren't a threat –

CHURCHILL. Why would they be threatened?

REITH. I am only allowed to broadcast news at seven p.m. because they fear for sales if I do earlier. You are creating a competitor which –

CHURCHILL. I appealed to their patriotism of course.

REITH. Ahhhh.

CHURCHILL. They're all frightened – and they are right to be – about the red threat – I told them my paper would ensure that the Great British public wouldn't get swept up in something it shouldn't.

REITH. Right.

CHURCHILL. And – to be honest – I didn't give them much of a choice. I commandeered. The *Morning Post*. For a start.

REITH. I'm afraid I won't be able to record it. Your *Gazette* going to press –

CHURCHILL. May I ask why not?

REITH. Because it won't make good listening.

CHURCHILL. You need the spot for your barbaric *Women's Hour* –

REITH. And because it'll be seen as an endorsement. There are those that are angry that the Government –

CHURCHILL. An endorsement?

REITH. It'll align the *Gazette* and the BBC.

CHURCHILL. And that would be wrong?

REITH. We have always tried to keep our news coverage non-partisan. Whereas the *Gazette*. If I've understood correctly… Well, tell me, what do you intend to report? During this strike? Does their side get a look-in?

Beat. CHURCHILL *assesses* REITH.

CHURCHILL. I do not agree that the TUC have as much right as the Government to news at this time. It is a much more difficult task to feed the nation than it is to wreck it. Don't you think? I do not believe it is *partisan* to not want this strike extended. Do you?

REITH. Of course not.

CHURCHILL. Then we are on the same team. A glory. Working together to bring compromise to this unfortunate division. I'll ask a final time – I'm not afraid of humiliation – you're sure you don't wish to hear my printing presses?

REITH. I appreciate the idea. But no.

CHURCHILL. Know your own mind, I can see that. Wonderful thing, I'm sure. Never had the sensation myself. Always prepared to listen to the advice of others.

REITH. What advice were you given about re-entering the Gold Standard? About the damage that could do? About the damage it did do to our economy?

CHURCHILL *looks at him carefully.*

CHURCHILL. I invited all sides to a dinner. I served goose. But that Keynes fellow – he couldn't quite convince me and the others – well, the benefits sounded most conducive. You think it was a mistake, I presume?

REITH. It seems to me you know your own mind well enough, Mr Churchill.

Beat.

CHURCHILL. Chess player, you're a chess player, planting the thought in my head. That I was somehow in the wrong. Well done, Mr Reith. Impressive.

Beat.

The scar?

REITH. Bullet went through my cheek.

CHURCHILL. Going over the top?

REITH. Trench inspection. I was in dress uniform and was caught out by a sniper. My first thought was that I'd been accidentally hit by a cricket ball. That's how it felt. My second was that I've spoilt a new tunic. 7th October 1915.

CHURCHILL. Unfortunate. Let's try to make sure we're not caught out on this one, shall we?

REITH. I don't intend to be.

CHURCHILL *nods and then exits.*

REITH *is left alone. He paces up and down. He turns on the radio.*

ELLA (*on radio*). I wouldn't say that's particularly barbaric, just simple household management –

He turns off the radio. He paces some more. ISABEL *enters.*

ISABEL. I'm sorry –

REITH. Has he gone?

ISABEL. I escorted him out myself. But he should never have been able to – I take full responsibility for him reaching you –

REITH. He couldn't be caged, I imagine?

ISABEL. I'm sorry, sir.

REITH. Please don't be. I know men like that. That'll be all.
Perhaps give me some quiet time for a moment –

ISABEL. Sir.

She exits. REITH *sits down.*

The world seems to tilt a moment.

CHARLIE. Johnnie…

Scene Six

The stage is full of action. London is created.

REITH. This is London and all stations calling.

Good morning, I welcome listeners back to the third day of
our coverage of the General Strike. The Prime Minister has
confirmed that the Government position remains the same –
no further negotiating until the General Strike is called off.
The TUC Council assembled at Eccleston Square this
morning. The outer door of the place of meeting was closed
and no pressmen were allowed in the hall.

BEVIN. We've got nothing. They're bleeding us dry.

PUGH. We have the people.

BEVIN. The 'people' are only just with us. And they're not all
behaving like one thing.

PUGH. *The British Worker* will spread our message and –

BEVIN. *The British Worker* cannot be printed or distributed in
sufficient numbers. Our message is being lost –

REITH. Excitement ran high at Canning Town and Poplar last
evening and the police met with considerable trouble. During
the afternoon and evening there were several rushes by
apparently organised gangs of youths near Poplar Hospital

but the police were able to deal with them. In Newcastle last night the rowdy element became so threatening that the volunteer drivers of buses, who have done good business in the absence of trams and trains, abandoned their vehicles. At Chesterly Street the crowd slashed the tyres of a bus driven by non-union labour. Central Station main entrances were invaded but the police rapidly cleared the premises.

CHURCHILL. Clemmie. Clemmie. Where's breakfast? Oh Christ, my head. Clemmie! CLEMMIE!

CLEMMIE. I am not your maid. I will not be summoned.

CHURCHILL. You're prettier than any maid. And *I* am summoned in my soul by *you*. For all time. I call you to ease my mind that you have not left me in the night.

CLEMMIE. You're still drunk.

CHURCHILL. I sadly have too fierce a hangover for that to be the case. You do look tremendous. You are tremendous.

CLEMMIE. Are you being safe with yourself?

CHURCHILL. I'm in my element.

CLEMMIE. You're drinking more.

CHURCHILL. Because I'm in my element. Fifty men blocked the North Road in Gosforth yesterday. Any motorist who succeeded in passing was stoned. A lorry carrying fish from Berwick was pulled up and the driver dragged from his seat. The lorry was overturned. The police arrived to break it up and found themselves pelted with rather good-quality salmon. It is times like this when leadership matters. I intend to matter. I'm in my element.

CLEMMIE *looks at him, concerned.*

CLEMMIE. No breakfast but here it is…

She has a copy of the British Gazette.

CHURCHILL. Oh my.

CLEMMIE. A rather shiny-faced young man delivered it. I think he'd rather expected me to let him up. He thought he might wake the great Winston Churchill with the smell of newsprint.

CHURCHILL. Not great. Just Winston Churchill.

CHURCHILL *leafs quickly through the newspaper.*
CLEMMIE *approaches the window.*

CLEMMIE. Oh what a sight.

CHURCHILL. You are a sight, this is a sight, what more sights can I need…

CLEMMIE. No. Winston. Come look. People are walking. Down the street. Hordes of them. They can't get the bus or the underground so they're walking to work. It's rather – magnificent.

CHURCHILL *gets out of bed and looks out of the window.*

CHURCHILL. Dear God, they look like an army. Marching towards – the future.

REITH. Finally, from me personally, the most noticeable feature of striking life in London today is the extraordinary congestion of the streets, particularly the great highways. We would ask every motor owner, before plunging into the stream of traffic, to consider rather carefully whether his journey is necessary. Both on foot and wheels. The Automobile Association also reminds us that owners of motorcars are expected to offer a lift to less fortunate pedestrians. It is on the foot-sore shop assistants and office girls that the industrial crisis falls heaviest. Keep a calm mind and a stout heart. Now over to the light orchestra in studio four who will be playing Brahms' 'String Quartet No. 1 in C minor'.

The Brahms is played.

PETER. And we're out.

REITH. Good.

PETER. 'Finally from me personally.' You are rather growing into this, aren't you?

REITH. Do I sound like a bore?

PETER. No. No. You're doing – admirably –

Beat.

I had a call this morning from the transmissions team at Daventry. Police officers have been posted there. I've noticed others too – there's two Peelers downstairs for that matter.

REITH. Yes, all matters I requested. Here. The roof of Selfridges. And especially Daventry. I told them Peter Eckersley's masterful transmission tower needs close guard. It informs the whole of Britain. Send your men up Borough Hill quick smart.

PETER (*unsure*). Thank you.

REITH (*reading something*). You seem – You have doubts?

PETER. They are not – they are not boxing us in? This Davidson and –

REITH. No. They are giving us value. And they are right to. We are doing great work here.

PETER *exits with a knowing look.* ISABEL *appears in his wake.*

ISABEL. Mr Reith, sir…

REITH. Ah. Yes.

ISABEL. That man Davidson is here again.

And your wife.

REITH *looks up.*

Scene Seven

MURIEL. I made you a jacket potato, and I bought a quarter of ham on the way in. The butcher's was ram-packed. I had to queue for forty minutes.

REITH *is a different man around his wife. More cautious. But there is love there.*

REITH. You're very kind.

MURIEL. I know you're not one for eating when – I know how your tummy can be.

REITH. It has presented me with no bother at all. As yet. Luckily.

She looks around the office.

MURIEL. Your mother telephoned. She seems determined to come down. Thinks you need her guidance.

REITH. She's tried here a few times.

MURIEL. You're lucky to have guards on the phone. I have no such luck.

REITH. She won't make it down. Not with the – Transport is quite a mess.

MURIEL. I told her you have me, and that you've been praying and that seemed to calm her. You have – been praying – haven't you?

REITH. I even made it out to a service at St Clement's yesterday. Took communion.

He looks at her, fragile now.

Have you listened? To the broadcasts?

MURIEL. Yes. They've been most educational. And you know I've always liked the sound of your voice. I'm pleased you're taking a lead – with the bulletins.

REITH. There's all sorts of pressures but I think I'm finding my way through.

MURIEL. Prayer will help with that.

REITH. Yes.

MURIEL. And I can – I'd – like you home.

REITH. Yes. A sleep in my bed will help matters.

MURIEL. What was it Charlie said about you? 'The problem with Johnnie is he's so tall that he doesn't see his feet.'

REITH *looks at her curiously.*

REITH. I always believed there was some great work for me to do in the world. I now believe this is it. And I think – Charlie would agree and I rather hope you would – you will.

MURIEL. I keep thinking – what if we had children in this – mess.

REITH. They will come soon enough.

MURIEL (*sharp*). That wasn't what I was saying.

REITH *looks at her carefully.*

REITH. Have you – liked what you heard? I've been making sure we've been saying exactly the right things.

MURIEL. What are the right things?

REITH. Have you liked it?

MURIEL. What do you expect me to say? It's terrifying. It sounds like the end of time. No.

REITH. But you can see the importance of it?

MURIEL. Why is it important for you to be important?

REITH (*irritated*). Did you come here just to criticise me?

MURIEL. I came here to give you some ham mostly. I queued for forty minutes.

REITH. William Noble, the chair of the committee that appointed me, said to me 'we're leaving it all to you' and they did – monthly check-ins but otherwise –

MURIEL. But if you wish for empty compliments I certainly can provide them –

REITH. There were thirty-six thousand licences when I started, there were four staff. Three-and-a-half years. That's all it's taken. And in that time I have transformed the BBC. They will soon give us a royal charter, did you know that? I have been promised it. No longer the British Broadcasting Company we will be the British Broadcasting Corporation. Britain's corporation. True prestige.

MURIEL. What a lot of words. What a lot of words you speak.

REITH. True influence. A guarantee of position for me and the BBC. The whole of Britain and we will represent it and this is our moment – my moment – to earn that trust and responsibility. I do not need empty compliments.

He looks at MURIEL, *who says nothing*.

Why did you mention Charlie?

CHARLIE. John. Johnnie.

MURIEL. Be careful of arrogance, Johnnie. And keep – you must keep praying. And come home. Please come home.

CHARLIE. What a head you have.

REITH. What a head I have?

MURIEL. What did you say? You're tired.

CHARLIE. I was just examining it. One can almost see the brains.

REITH. Brains of a bird.

CHARLIE. A big bird.

REITH. May we stay here forever?

CHARLIE. Forever.

REITH. Build a bivouac. Live out in the wild. Catch rabbits. Hunt deer.

CHARLIE. Have you been arrested for not returning to the army?

REITH. I don't feel scared in the trenches. Or I do and I don't notice it. And then I come home and my mother is there and expectation and –

CHARLIE. I have never known a man who expected as much from life as you.

REITH. All I want is this.

CHARLIE. But that's not true, Johnnie.

REITH. Promise me we'll always have this.

CHARLIE. I promise that I will always be there – for you – just as I hope you will always be there for me –

REITH. I will –

He lifts CHARLIE *to his feet. They stand close. Tender.*

I feel as though you are already lost to me.

CHARLIE. What brains you have in that head of yours. What fear.

REITH. I feel as though I must study your face, so as to carry it with me. That I cannot forget a single piece of you.

CHARLIE. You have my photo already.

REITH. Let us stay here tonight. Mother will not be concerned.

CHARLIE *looks at him gently.*

CHARLIE. I fear that is not what either of us need. Come on, dear chap. Chin up. Think of Jerusalem.

A fog grows.

REITH. I'll think of you.

CHARLIE. I like you just as you like me –

REITH. Charlie?

CHARLIE. I do, Johnnie.

Scene Eight

ISABEL. On day four of the strike, fog descended. A horrible dark and dank fog. That seemed to consume everyone.

The walks to work, the bonhomie, everything started to fade away as everyone was caught in the miserable great trek.

And then everyone is onstage, walking forward through the fog. It seems like a sea of people.

CHURCHILL. Good morning. Good morning.

ISABEL. There was a democracy to the misery. Though those in fancy cars still passed by – despite the dangers of them doing so. But there was such torment to it too. It cloaked the world.

BEVIN *is standing on a box as people walk by.*

BEVIN. We are not declaring war on the people. War has been declared by the Government pushed on by sordid capitalism. The problem of ownership draining dry our industry. Not just in mining. In all industries. We must challenge the notion that industry does not pay when the only reason it does not is the profiteering of those above us. We must challenge, challenge, challenge.

ISABEL. It cloaked those travelling from shop to shop to get whatever food they could. It cloaked those on the way to picket lines. It cloaked those taking jobs that would break the strike and it cloaked those desperate to prevent them doing so. It even cloaked the voices of the dispute, those desperate to have their words heard.

BEVIN. I, Ernest Bevin, Secretary of the Transport and General Workers' Union, elected by you all to represent your best interests, I rely as we rely on every man and woman – on all of you – to fight for the soul of the labour movement and the salvation of the miners. Solidarity has meaning if it is truly solid.

CHURCHILL. Good morning. Good morning.

ISABEL. And within that cloak, something felt different. Something was changing. Shifting. Altering.

BEVIN. Brothers and sisters, comrades, they are doing all they can to deny us means of amplification, so it is you who must take our message and spread it far and wide. The red flag flies through your mouths.

REITH *sits in front of a microphone*.

REITH. Regent's Park was closed to the public this morning, every entrance being guarded. Victoria Park has been taken over by the military authorities and is now being utilised as a military encampment.

There have been reports of disturbances at Woolwich and Camberwell. As regards the former, they are without foundation. At Camberwell Green there was a slight disturbance last night, and four policemen received minor injuries.

And there's the fog. The plague of darkness has been added to the other nine plagues from which London is suffering today. But nothing can quench the indomitable cockney sense of humour.

A shadowy light rises on HELENA MILLAIS.

HELENA MILLAIS. Ullo, me ducks, 'ere I am again with me old string bag and nothing to sing bar 'Ours Is a Nice 'Ouse Ours Is'.

REITH. We trust we shan't be thought to be underrating the gravity of the present situation if we drop into the same mood.

We heard today about a cheerful young person who had only driven a car before – once – but seeing a handsome-looking vehicle for sale, price thirty pounds, she bought it and set out for Whitehall – to help the Government. Somewhere in Piccadilly a cheerful policeman held a large white gauntlet across her path. By a superhuman effort she managed to stop. The hand dropped in due course but the car would not start. The traffic behind hooted more and more furiously.

Then the cheerful policeman drew from his mouth a large piece of toffee which he was sucking and held it enticingly in front of the bonnet or the car. And at that moment – believe it or not! – the car started forward!

This is London. And now it's time for *Children's Hour.* So let's find out what Jennings has been up to this week.

The recording light goes out.

REITH *stands and stretches out his back. There is something vaguely ominous about how he does so. Something sad.*

PETER. What knowledge have you that the events in Woolwich were without foundation…

REITH. I was informed.

PETER. By the Government.

REITH. News is the gathering of information from all pertinent sources, Peter, the Government is a pretty crucial source.

PETER. And what of the four police officers injured in Camberwell Green? I assure you that means forty strikers were injured in the same attack.

REITH. I have no reports of that.

PETER. Then should we not try and find out the truth before stating it as if it were truth.

REITH. We know enough, we know officers were injured, you aren't claiming we aren't on the side of the police in this? Of law and order? Of decency –

PETER. Decency? Have you any idea how these people are living?

REITH. Of course I do. I do not live in a gilded cage. I'll remind you I served alongside many working men. But that has little to do with –

PETER. Five or six to a room. No heat. Holes in the floor and the walls. And if you want to use a lavatory…

REITH. We've all had to live with an outside privy.

PETER. A five-minute walk through fetid land carrying a
bucket with you to wash away whatever filth you find.

REITH. I'm not sure the Latin is quite necessary, Peter.

PETER. There's disease. There's severe malnutrition. There's
no medical care. This strike is them fighting for their lives.

REITH. No. This strike is them fighting for the miners. And
perhaps keeping failing industry open through continuous
subsidy is not the be-all and end-all they presume it is. Did
you know nearly three-quarters of the coal produced in the
last quarter of 1925 cost more to get out of the ground than it
was worth on the market? And that is not from the *Gazette*,
that is from an in-depth report on this very station –

PETER. And why is it not profitable? For one: land rent. Do
you know how much the Duke of Northumberland made
from his land last year? Seventy-three thousand pounds –

REITH. So now we deny landowners their mineral rights?
You're sounding like a Soviet –

PETER. For two: an overvalued pound. Because our Chancellor
re-entered the Gold Standard at an overvalued rate. Polish
and American coal is cheaper than ours because their
currency is cheaper –

REITH. Peter, that is a question of policy – a debate the
Government is having –

PETER. A debate we *hope* they are. Because the British people
certainly aren't. Because the unions can't get their opinion
out because they have no access to paper, printer or a
microphone. I don't need you to agree with me about what
has afflicted coal, whether it's money-grabbing landowners,
or an inflated Gold Standard or simply that the industry is no
longer economically viable. I merely think that the country
has the right to have the same disagreement. The task of
news is to arm people to make their decisions and that means
knowing all sides.

And that's an argument with power.

Have you heard of the Q Division?

REITH. The who?

PETER. Fascists who've decided it's their duty to break this strike. They are more vicious than the military. Than the special constables. Some young men were picking coal off the railway track last night. I saw them set upon by these fascists. They were left insensible. And will we ever report this? Of course we won't. Because the Government is grateful for their work even if it won't ever endorse it. That is who we're inspiring, John.

REITH *wobbles, clearly upset by this.*

What you've – we've built here in three-and-a-half years is a marvel, and it is a marvel precisely because the public trusts us. But that trust will only go so far. If we broadcast only that which presents the Government side, and nothing which presents the strikers. It's partiality by elimination. They're already calling us the British Falsehood Company. They think we've ceded control. Please. For all our sakes. You can't let that continue.

And this really hits home. REITH *thinks. His struggle riven through him.*

REITH. The Prime Minister is making a statement tonight.

PETER. On our wireless no doubt?

REITH. As is right. He is a reasonable man. I will talk to him about – Maybe I can talk to him about…

PETER. Maybe you can.

REITH *looks up, his jaw steeled.*

REITH. I will set this ship right, Peter, you will see.

Scene Nine

REITH*'s home living room.* PETER, STANLEY BALDWIN,
REITH *and* DAVIDSON *hover around a microphone.*

ISABEL. For some reason on that fateful night, Mr Reith
decided – perhaps in a display of power, perhaps in a display
of something else entirely – that the Prime Minister should
broadcast from John's own home. I do think he enjoyed the
fact that his wife could see the Prime Minister attending on
him. Yes, it was probably a display of power.

BALDWIN. And perhaps I think I might like to finish with
something personal –

REITH *is reading pages from a prepared statement.*

REITH. What about something about peace?

BALDWIN. Splendid idea.

Beat.

What about peace?

REITH. You could say you are a man of peace, that you are
longing and working and praying for peace –

DAVIDSON. – but that you will not compromise the dignity of
the British constitution.

REITH. You misunderstand, I rather meant peace for all.

BALDWIN. Well, I like that combination. Peace and the
constitution. Have you a legible hand, Reith? Might you
write something for me –

REITH *hesitates.* MURIEL *steps in.*

MURIEL. Yes. He has a fine hand.

She smiles at BALDWIN.

BALDWIN. So wonderful when our wives have faith in us,
isn't it, Mr Reith?

REITH. Yes, sir.

REITH *begins to write.* DAVIDSON *approaches his shoulder.*

DAVIDSON. Thinking about it. Not sure about 'dignity'. Perhaps – 'safety' or 'security' – might seem –

BALDWIN. I will not compromise – no, I will not surrender the security of the British constitution for that constitution is bigger than I, bigger, indeed, than any of us. Et cetera.

REITH. Sir, but if your appeal could be wider – to –

BALDWIN. So I am to just talk into –

REITH. It's just like talking to a neighbour.

BALDWIN. I try not to talk to my neighbours. Winston lives at number eleven, after all.

MURIEL. Ha! How funny.

PETER. It's nine twenty-eight, it's time, sir.

REITH. I will introduce you –

BALDWIN. Good.

REITH *sits. He looks at* MURIEL, *then he looks at* PETER, *who looks back.*

REITH. Can I just though – Before you – You will be heard by the whole country tonight. What the BBC does best is serve both third and first class as if they're equal. It's all the same, you see. The service does not differ.

BALDWIN. A government hopes to be the same.

REITH. If we seem to be controlled, they won't forgive us, or you. The BBC is soon to be a national asset, sir, and –

PETER. Thirty seconds. Shall I put the feed through –

REITH. Yes.

PETER *presses a switch.* SANDY POWELL *appears.*

SANDY POWELL. There's this bribing you know and there's a lot of it going on believe me. A fella tried to bribe me only last week.

REITH. Sandy Powell. This is his goalkeeper sketch. Very
funny man.

SANDY POWELL. He came up and said Sandy, I'll give you
fifty pounds to lose this match. I said no I wouldn't do a thing
like that, I said I'm going to play my usual game. He said well
that'll do and it will save me fifty quid. I've been Sandy
Powell, you've been wonderful, see you next week.

REITH *looks at* BALDWIN *desperately.* PETER *signals.*

REITH. London and all stations calling – this is the BBC, and
now – the Prime Minister.

BALDWIN *looks at* REITH *– who signals.*

BALDWIN. Good evening.

The General Strike has now been in progress for nearly a
week, and I think that, as Prime Minister, I should tell the
nation once more what is at stake in the lamentable struggle
that is going on.

What is the issue for which the Government is fighting? It is
fighting because, while negotiations were still in progress,
the Trade Union Council ordered a General Strike,
presumably to try and force Parliament and the community
to bend to its will. With that object, the Trade Union Council
has decided that the railways shall not run, that transport
shall not move, unloading of ships shall stop and that no
news shall reach the public. Can there be a more direct attack
upon the community than that a body not elected by the
voters of the country, without consulting the people, without
consulting even the Trade Unionists, and in order to impose
conditions never yet defined, should dislocate the life of the
nation and try to starve us into submission?

He pauses. He looks around the room.

The Government's position is simple – the General Strike
must be called off absolutely and without reserve. The
mining industry dispute can then be settled up. This is a fair
arrangement and it would be a thousand times better to

accept it than to continue a struggle which can only increase misery and disaster the longer it lasts.

The laws of England are the people's birthright. These laws are in your keeping. You have made Parliament your guardian. This General Strike called by these revolutionary forces is a challenge to Parliament and is the road to anarchy and ruin.

I am your Prime Minister and a man of peace. I am living, working and praying for peace. But I will not surrender the security of the British constitution for that constitution is bigger than I, bigger, indeed, than any of us. Thank you for listening.

PETER. And we're back to studio two.

BALDWIN. Well, that went well, I suppose.

MURIEL. I thought it was very moving.

BALDWIN. Mrs Reith, I have long believed England rests in the conscience of our housewives. Your confidence means a huge amount to me.

Beat. PETER *looks at* REITH.

REITH. There are those that say that the Government cut off negotiations first, sir.

BALDWIN. Sorry?

REITH. Correct me if I'm wrong but in your speech just now you said the TUC forced you into it whilst the negotiations were still ongoing –

BALDWIN. This is true.

REITH. But is it not also true that the Government stopped negotiating with the TUC because the *Daily Mail* workers refused to print an editorial condemning them. Something the TUC had no knowledge of… and once the Government ceased negotiating the leadership felt they'd no other choice but to –

BALDWIN. These matters are always so difficult. And the stories so confused.

REITH. This is not a time for dope, even if the people could be doped. The hostile would be made more hostile from resentment –

BALDWIN. Yes indeed, we must come not between the dragon and his wrath. *Lear. King.*

REITH. Most of the good things in this world are badly distributed and most people have to go without them. But the wireless… The BBC. It does not matter how many thousands may be listening, there is always enough for others. The genius and the fool, the wealthy and the poor listen as one. It makes the nation one man.

BALDWIN. If the nation were one man it would make my life considerably easier, Mr Reith.

REITH. I'm not a politician, I'm a broadcaster, people need to always trust we tell the truth. We don't wish to extend the strike. But equally, the BBC can't be seen to be on the Government's side, you understand? We can't pick either side.

BALDWIN. Interesting…

REITH. How so?

BALDWIN. Wouldn't you say you just have? Picked a side? Wasn't that what tonight was?

BALDWIN *picks up the* Daily Telegraph.

I told them, you know – I made very clear – the strike will only make the situation worse for them – it will become impossible for me to resist pressure from within my party to rescind trade union privileges.

REITH. We're all held to ransom.

BALDWIN. Well, no, I wouldn't put it so starkly.

His face changes.

Ransom, maybe that is it? Blooming... S and then M. It does fit. Clue was redemptive. Ransom. Sneaky buggers. Do you crossword?

REITH. No.

BALDWIN. *Telegraph* is the one that always consumes me. Old copy, of course, but keeping me going with their fiendish ways.

REITH. Yes.

BALDWIN. Still, good exercise for the brain I've always thought. Well, thanks again, Mr Reith.

BALDWIN *exits*.

PETER *looks at* REITH.

REITH. Daventry calling... Dark and still,
    The dead men sleep at the foot of the hill.
    The dark tree, set on the height by the Dane,
    Stands like a sentry over the slain.
    Bowing his head above their tomb,
    Till trumpet rends the seals of doom.
    Earth has forgotten their ancient wars.
    But the lone tree rises against the stars,
    Whispering, 'Here in my heart I keep,
    Mysteries, deep as the world is deep.
    Deeper far then the world ye know,
    Is the world through which my voices go'...

Scene Ten

Rain falls on one side of the stage. And from within it comes a noise. Comes MEN *and* WOMEN, *cowed and beaten.*

REITH *appears in the rain, he looks forlorn.*

REITH *passes a* WOMAN *walking through the rain. She's coughing.*

REITH. Are you quite well?

WOMAN. Sir. Yes, sir. Can't stop, sir.

REITH. Why can't you? You'll give yourself consumption.

WOMAN. I've messages to deliver, sir, for the strike authority – sir.

She coughs, for a long period of time. REITH *takes out his handkerchief and hands it her. She takes it from him.*

REITH. Your hand – is black and blue.

WOMAN. Some don't like what I deliver, do they?

REITH. You must get home.

WOMAN. What business is it of yours what I do? I know men like you.

REITH. Then – take my umbrella at least. Keep the rain from doing any more damage.

He gives her the umbrella.

WOMAN. How much is it worth?

REITH. I would not – know.

WOMAN. Can I have the money instead, sir? Give us a bob, sir. I've children to feed.

REITH. You've children to feed and you're out doing this?

WOMAN. I've children to feed and I've no choice but to do this.

REITH hesitates and then takes out his wallet. He gives her a ten-bob note.

REITH. Use it for essentials…

WOMAN. What do you think I'd use it for, sir?

She moves on.

REITH. May I ask – how do you live?

WOMAN. Well as we can.

REITH. Do you share a bathroom with many?

WOMAN (*with scorn*). The beak on you. Take this. You might learn something.

REITH *reluctantly takes the leaflet.*

ALL. Daventry calling
Daventry calling

CHURCHILL. Jix. Jix.

JIX. Tremendous rain today. It's slowed recruitment considerably.

CHURCHILL. Tremendous rain today. It's slowed the pickets too. We'll soon compel more for you. I'm commandeering the WH Smith distribution centre today.

JIX. Planting your flag in poor old WH.

CHURCHILL. Did you hear the Prime Minister last night?

JIX. I don't have a wireless.

CHURCHILL. Marvellous he was, Jix. Marvellous.

JIX. The liberals are going to give you a hard time today. In the Commons. They're angry you're denying them a voice.

CHURCHILL. Let them. I was once a liberal. I know how they roar.

The rain stops as REITH *steps into Savoy Hill.*

ISABEL. You're wet through…

He looks at her, his mind resolved.

REITH. And I sought for a man among them, that they should make up the hedge, and stand in the gap before me for the land, that I should not destroy it: but I found none.

ISABEL. Yes, Mr Reith?

REITH. Ezekiel 22:30.

ISABEL. I don't know what it means.

REITH. Reports of attacks in Hammersmith and Poplar last night. I want us to know for ourselves whether there's any truth to them. Who have we placed in the field? Darnell and Chapman, tell them I need more than I'm getting.

ISABEL. Yes, sir.

CHURCHILL *runs after* BALDWIN.

CHURCHILL. Prime Minister. Prime Minister. Prime Minister. I wanted to congratulate you on a most excellent radio broadcast.

BALDWIN. Thank you, Winston.

CHURCHILL. And I wanted to tell you that I've had it transcribed and it will be running in our *Gazette*.

BALDWIN. They are going after you in the House today.

CHURCHILL. So everyone keeps saying. Let them.

BALDWIN. You won't attend?

CHURCHILL. I intended to.

BALDWIN. I feel your talents might be better spent elsewhere. Let them shout into their paper bag. That's my advice.

As he speaks, REITH *carefully takes the sodden leaflet out of his pocket and spreads it on his desk.*

REITH. In other news, official Government denial is given to rumours that serious disturbances occurred this morning at Hammersmith, Putney, Chiswick and Poplar. The BBC awaits confirmation of this.

A fine story of discipline and loyalty comes to us from a London Elementary School. Owing to traffic difficulties one morning this week the whole staff were late, but on arrival they found that the senior boys had assembled the school in the hall, taken prayers, and marched the younger boys to their classrooms. The fathers of these boys are mostly labourers and are mostly out on strike. There is no need to emphasise the moral of this story.

He pauses a moment. He thinks. He knows this is a moment of extreme bravery.

Finally, the *British Gazette* was the subject of a discussion in the Commons this afternoon on the motion for the adjournment. Commander Kenworthy, Liberal, alleged that the newspaper of which he understood Mr Churchill was the editor, was not publishing a fair summary of the proceedings in Parliament.

BALDWIN, DAVIDSON *and* CHURCHILL *come closer to listen.*

He said, and I quote: 'When you have an official paper, you have to be extraordinarily careful really to speak the truth, in the first place, and, secondly, not to give isolated bits of information and put them forward in an attempt to influence public opinion...

COMMANDER KENWORTHY. You should confine yourself to news, and above all you should not put in anything of a nature to inflame passions at this time.

MEMBERS OF THE HOUSE. Hear hear.

REITH. Mr Jack Jones supported Commander Kenworthy's plea, declaring that the Government was using public money to libel Trade Unionists. Mr Churchill was not present at the debate. The House adjourned at four o'clock.

This is London. And now to over to Sandy Powell for another important broadcast.

The recording light switches off. REITH *sits back.*

PETER. And we're out. Crumbs. Well done.

REITH. He won't like it.

PETER. You just said his precious paper was a rag. He'll hate it.

CHURCHILL. What did he just say? DID YOU JUST HEAR THAT?

REITH *stands up and prowls around the room like a lion. Clearly pleased with himself.*

On the British Broadcasting Company. The British. You hear him? On the British Broadcasting –

REITH. I was simply repeating what was said in the Commons.

PETER. You simply have made sure everyone *heard* what was said in the Commons. Well done, John. Well done.

REITH *looks up as* CHARLIE *comes in.*

CHARLIE. The world was all before them, where to choose
Their place of rest, and Providence their guide;
They, hand in hand, with wandering steps and slow,
Through Eden took their solitary way.

REITH. Yes, yes, it is good, yes, control has been retaken.

PETER. A war has been begun, more like.

Beat.

REITH. Yes, we're now – back in control.

Interval.

At some point during the interval, a man should walk onstage playing SANDY POWELL. *He has a ukulele and he is not afraid to play it.*

He strums and then he stops, and then he strums and sings.

SANDY POWELL. A famous dog once came to town
    Known to his friends as Pete
    His pedigree was ten yards long
    His looks were hard to beat

    And as he trotted down the road
    'Twas beautiful to see
    His work at every corner
    Every post and every tree

    He never missed a landmark
    He never missed a post
    For piddling was his masterpiece
    And piddling pleased him most

    The city dogs stood looking on
    In deep and jealous rage
    To see this little country dog
    The piddler of his age

    They smelt his efforts one by one
    They smelt him two by two
    But noble Pete in high disdain
    Stood still till they were through

    Then when they'd smelt him everywhere
    The praise for him ran high
    But when one smelt him underneath
    Pete piddled in his eye

    Just then to show these city dogs
    He didn't care a damn
    He strolled into the grocer's shop
    And piddled on the ham

He piddled on the cornflakes
He piddled on the floor
And when the grocer threw him out
He piddled up the door

Behind him all the city dogs
Debated what to do
They'd hold a piddling carnival
The hoop they'd put him through

They showed him all the piddling posts
They knew about the town
And off they set with many a wink
To wear the stranger down

But Pete was with them all the way
With vigour and with vim
A thousand piddles more or less
Were all the same to him

And on and on went noble Pete
As tireless as a windmill
And very soon those city dogs
Were piddled to a standstill

Then Pete an exhibition gave
Of all the ways to piddle
With double drips and fancy flips
And now and then a dribble

The city dogs said farewell Pete
Your piddling did defeat us
But no one ever put them wise
That Pete… had diabetes.

He stops. He looks around.

Put that on your radio, Mr Reith.

He walks offstage.

ACT TWO

Scene One

In studio three, a very loud man is declaiming loudly into a microphone.

CORNWALL. HOW NOOOW BROWN COW. THE RICH WITCH WON A WRISTWATCH, WHICH WATCH DID THE RICH WITCH WIN. AHA. AHA. AHA. BECAUSE I WOULD NOT SEE THY CRUEL NAILS PLUCK OUT HIS POOR OLD EYES; AHA AHA AHA NOR THY FIERCE SISTER IN HIS ANNOINTED FLESH STICK BOARISH FANGS. BOARISH FANGS. BOARISH FANGS. FANGS. FANGS. F-F-F-FANGS.

ENGINEER. A couple of points, if I may.

CORNWALL. Not to worry, I won't overenunciate like that, just getting the lips and teeth nice and roasting. FANGS. F-F-FANGS.

ENGINEER. Second point, perhaps you might stand further from the microphone?

CORNWALL. I want to be sure they can hear me?

ENGINEER. They will hear you.

CORNWALL. Not just what I say you understand, but HOW I SAY IT. AHA.

ENGINEER. They will hear you. Now a few cues to talk about before we go on air. The floor is gravel we've decided and Gerry here will be doing your walking.

GERRY *walks in a tray full of cat litter. He has a spade attached to a belt around his waist.*

CORNWALL. Morning, Gerry. Wonderful walk. May I ask a question though…

ENGINEER. Is it about his sword?

CORNWALL. That's a spade.

ENGINEER. Not on the wireless it isn't.

CORNWALL. Oh how delightful. Attack, brave gardeners, attack.

ENGINEER. Gardens are where we get a lot of our – you know the sound we use for breaking bones?

CORNWALL. You simply must tell me.

ENGINEER. We snap some celery.

They both laugh.

CORNWALL. The eyeball gouging?

ENGINEER. We've been experimenting with that for this – we thought we'd try a sharpened teaspoon entering an overripe plum.

CORNWALL. Delightful.

ENGINEER. And then Gloucester – well, he'll vomit afterwards which is just the release of a sponge into a bucket. It'll be hugely effective.

CORNWALL. It already sounds it.

ISABEL. By day six of the strike chaos ruled. Buses with barbed wires sluiced through streets down which on one side people screamed 'God save the King' and on the other 'the red flag'. Lorries were chained to railway lines to prevent blackleg strike-breakers and the police armed themselves for war.

PETER *enters the room.*

ENGINEER. Oh, sir, uh, do you need the space?

PETER. No. No. I just came here to – I just came here to watch – if that's agreeable – to you both.

CORNWALL. More than agreeable. I'm Cornwall. I'm playing Cornwall. And you are?

ENGINEER. This is Peter Eckersley. He built this station.

PETER. John Reith built this station.

CORNWALL. The finest place for Shakespeare that ever existed. His words work while your mind races.

PETER. Please – carry on –

CORNWALL. I was just – warming my vocals whilst the Earl of Gloucester and my wife are in the toilet. Quite a time, all this. The winds are blowing, what?

ISABEL. I watched a young boy moving from house to house begging for scraps. They had nothing for him. His cries for Christian charity grew more insistent and one kindly woman found him a crust of bread. He took the crust with delight and ran down the street with it. To where his mother and two baby sisters waited for him. They carefully shared the crust between them, making sure not to lose one crumb. Marches. Misery. And us ploughing our furrow through it.

CHARLIE. Let us carve our names…

REITH. It will damage the bench.

CHARLIE *laughs*.

Someone paid for this bench, Charlie. For others to enjoy. I don't think it's fair that we destroy it.

CHARLIE. And I don't think it's fair that you're such a stick-in-the-mud – but there you are, it is as it is.

REITH. You're cruel to me.

CHARLIE. It will simply transform the bench. Into a monument. For how we feel about each other.

REITH. Will it?

CHARLIE. And in years to come they will ask 'Who was John Reith and who was Charlie Bowser?'

REITH. Maybe they'll know our names in years to come.

CHARLIE. You are the sweetest thing.

REITH. I'm nothing of the kind.

CHARLIE. No, you're a hardened war veteran.

> CHARLIE *gently and intimately touches* REITH*'s face.*

> And yet your face doesn't feel hard at all. It must be that the air is somehow softer up there.

REITH. I'm not much taller than you.

CHARLIE. Softer and kinder. Now, I need to tell you, I've met someone I think you'll like.

REITH. Have you?

CHARLIE. She's funny, she's bright, she has a great set of pins.

REITH. Sounds like she ticks all the boxes.

CHARLIE. Well, she does rather, for me at least.

REITH (*what?*). For you?

CHARLIE. Yes. What of that?

> REITH *looks at him strangely.*

> Perhaps – I was thinking – perhaps I'll ask her to marry me.

REITH. You won't.

CHARLIE. I may.

REITH. But we are – you and I are – not the marrying kind.

CHARLIE. You've never considered marriage?

REITH. No.

CHARLIE. Why not?

> REITH *walks forward towards* CHARLIE.

REITH. Because I am satisfied in my relationship with you.

CHARLIE. Well, I hope I will marry… and I'm thinking – I'm seriously considering – I'm thinking I will marry her.

> REITH *cannot digest this shock.*

REITH. Charlie. Please. Do you think what we have and marriage are – compatible?

CHARLIE. Oh Johnnie. They have to be.

REITH *turns this over and over in his mind.*

REITH. What's she called?

CHARLIE. Muriel.

MURIEL *is lit at the back of the stage, there's something vaguely ghostlike about her.*

REITH. Who?

MURIEL. Oh good, you're home.

CHARLIE. You'll like her, Johnnie. You will.

REITH. I'm tired. I thought I might – go straight to sleep.

MURIEL. Would you have a cup of tea with me first?

REITH. Another time.

MURIEL. Johnnie –

CHARLIE. Johnnie – where have you gone?

REITH. Muriel, you tell me to rest, I'm here to rest –

MURIEL. Might I – I thought I might stay in your room with you tonight – provide you with –

She walks up to him. And he looks at her, so humble.

CHARLIE. I don't like you like this –

MURIEL. Make sure you sleep. You know how restless you are on your own.

CHARLIE. I can see your anger and I don't like it –

REITH. A kind offer.

CHARLIE. Johnnie, I need you to promise me you'll think this through – properly – for me –

MURIEL. You don't need for – anything?

REITH *looks at her, and we see what's inside him.*

REITH. Perhaps we could pray together?

MURIEL. I'd like that.

He holds out a hand to her. And kneels. She kneels beside him.

Scene Two

The offices of 10 Downing Street. CHURCHILL *arrives through an interconnecting door.* BALDWIN *is surrounded, as always, with the doers of government.*

CHURCHILL. Prime Minister, I understand you've turned down my convoy protection request.

BALDWIN. Ah yes, I decided machine guns lining the route might be unnecessary.

CHURCHILL. I'll settle for tanks.

BALDWIN. Winston –

CHURCHILL. Stanley, one does wonder how someone as humourless as you rose to such a level.

BALDWIN. Perhaps humour is not the be-all and end-all you think it is.

CHURCHILL. Perhaps.

BALDWIN. And you were being serious – were you not – about the machine guns – ?

CHURCHILL *checks* BALDWIN*'s face.*

CHURCHILL. Well, yes. I may have been.

BALDWIN. In what way did you think they might help the problem?

CHURCHILL. A visual statement. Of intent. From us to them. The convoy will run from the coast to central London and I will line the route with photographers and we will place it on the front page of the *British Gazette*.

BALDWIN. You think it'll make good press?

CHURCHILL. I think it'll reflect well on us all. I'm grateful for you reconsidering it. If that is what you're doing.

BALDWIN. I must get back to my office. Another time, perhaps?

CHURCHILL. I – have not seen action.

BALDWIN. On what?

CHURCHILL. Wuthering Heights and his withering broadcasts.

BALDWIN. You're referring to John Reith? Wuthering Heights? Very dry.

CHURCHILL. Have you heard him? He sounds like an ambitious West End actor impersonating a French university lecturer addressing English students.

BALDWIN. I understand your personal distaste. But Davidson is policing him.

CHURCHILL. Then he is not policing him tightly enough. For he seems to spend the entire time libelling me.

BALDWIN. I heard. It was merely one bulletin.

CHURCHILL. Did he show you it in advance, Davidson?

DAVIDSON. No. But it isn't libellous repeating what was said in the House.

CHURCHILL. My apologies, it's treacherous. Kenworthy blah blah blah 'alleged that the newspaper of which he understood Mr Churchill was the editor, was not publishing a fair summary of the proceedings in Parliament'. He was calling my paper discriminatory and partisan. On the BBC.

BALDWIN. I did not like it either. But he hasn't put anything on air as provocative since. I rather expect he is waiting for us to react.

CHURCHILL. Then let's surprise him by doing so. Prime Minister, I think it is monstrous not to use an instrument such as the BBC in a moment such as this to best possible advantage –

DAVIDSON. Anger is not the answer here.

CHURCHILL. My question is of the Prime Minister, not his apparatchik. Surely as Chancellor of the Exchequer I deserve his words.

BALDWIN *nods. He pours a glass of water, he drinks it.*

BALDWIN. The *Gazette* keeps commandeering more facilities, I hear.

CHURCHILL. Only that which is not being used.

DAVIDSON. The Angus Brass, Somerset House, Phoenix Wharf… Quite an empire.

CHURCHILL. Simply a necessary one. I've tried to requisition all the paper and ink they use to print the *British Worker*. Are you avoiding the question or ruminating on it because if ruminating I have further argument…

BALDWIN. You can't have your machine guns and you can't have the BBC.

CHURCHILL. May I ask why not?

BALDWIN. Because it's not good politics. I want victory as much as you do, Winston. But it'll achieve nothing if we are seen to bully. Some don't, but many still trust the BBC and that is very useful indeed.

CHURCHILL. 'Bully' is a strong word, I would rather use the word 'control'…

BALDWIN. He's had his rebellion. It did little damage, bar a little bruising of you. Now we've seen his stripes we can control him better.

CHURCHILL. And if you're wrong?

BALDWIN *pauses. He looks up at* CHURCHILL *coldly.*

BALDWIN. Inside. You may stay, Davidson. You are not some prophet –

CHURCHILL. I never claimed –

BALDWIN. Leading us to a promised land of milk and honey –

CHURCHILL. The milk storage in Hyde Park does seem to be working. They've called it a lake, have you heard?

BALDWIN. This situation is complicated –

CHURCHILL. It is a situation they created and you have not yet controlled. *Prime* Minister.

This is dangerous and they both know it.

BALDWIN. Perhaps there is a gold standard of labour relations I should be consulting –

CHURCHILL. Back to that brush to beat me with?

BALDWIN. You tire of it?

CHURCHILL. I shackled us to discipline. Shackled us to reality. I fully expect it to work after a small adjustment or two, and I would have expected it to work sooner were it not for inflationary governmental decisions in other departments that weren't encouraged to apply fiscal discipline –

BALDWIN. This is my fault? My mess?

CHURCHILL. You may blame me for a few teething problems in *my* restoration of the Gold Standard, what I would say in return is that perhaps we might have seen greater success had *your* Government properly supported it.

BALDWIN. The Gallipoli offensive too, perhaps? Was I responsible for that? Two hundred and fifty thousand casualties…

CHURCHILL looks at him regally, they both know that was a low blow.

CHURCHILL. The other brush, played cheaply, remind me to play you at draw poker, you must have little talent for it.

I believe I can claim – I believe I have claimed responsibility for Gallipoli and asked for forgiveness. Have you never made a mistake?

BALDWIN. Perhaps not as many as you.

CHURCHILL *stares at him for a moment.*

CHURCHILL. I believed Gallipoli would win us the war. As First Lord of the Admiralty, I believed we could take it, and I thought it might gain us control of the crucial Ottoman straits. I was wrong. I know the lives I cost. But I am not – I am not – wrong about this. May I remind you the Soviet Communists are gathering at the door just waiting for us to open it even a crack. And they do not recognise the word 'bully'. Just that of victor and vanquished.

He exits.

DAVIDSON. You gave him last word?

BALDWIN. He simply stole it, and I let him. Drink? I didn't offer one earlier for fear he'd drain me dry.

DAVIDSON *laughs.*

DAVIDSON. I've recently become unsure whether that isn't inflated as well, for effect.

BALDWIN. He wants to appear a drunkard?

DAVIDSON. He wants to appear extraordinary.

Beat.

He sees the whole strike affair as a film producer would see it, with this difference. Film producers do not act; Winston intends to appear as the hero of the story himself.

BALDWIN. And you're sure John Reith isn't cut from the same cloth?

DAVIDSON. It's possible. Yet, I'm sure, with some gentle persuasion…

BALDWIN. He is right, about the Soviets, they do watch us, with intent. Do what you must. Don't let Reith goad us again.

DAVIDSON. Yes, Prime Minister.

Scene Three

REITH*'s office.* AMELIA *is reading from a sheet in front of her.*

AMELIA. When the present strike is ended, His Majesty's Government will take effectual measures to prevent the victimisation by trades unions of any man who remains at work or may return to work.

DAVIDSON *enters the room.* REITH *notices.*

Every man who does his duty loyally to the country in the present crisis will be protected from loss of trade union benefit, superannuation allowances or pensions. His Majesty's Government will take whatever steps are necessary in Parliament or otherwise for this purpose.

DAVIDSON. Shall we delete 'in Parliament or otherwise'?

AMELIA *looks at* REITH, *who nods.*

AMELIA. His Majesty's Government will take whatever steps necessary for this purpose.

DAVIDSON. Wonderful.

REITH *nods and then indicates to* AMELIA *to read on.*

DAVIDSON *walks over and opens* REITH*'s drinks cabinet. A whisky is poured.*

AMELIA. In Croydon a platelayer was sentenced to two months' hard labour for threatening volunteer workers with a stolen hammer.

DAVIDSON. Not sure we need Mr Platelayer. The hammer makes it rather too graphic.

REITH. No. We'll keep the hammer.

She looks at REITH, *who looks at* DAVIDSON, *who nods*.

AMELIA. It is reported that a section of printers at Hinckley today returned to work. In a letter to their union they state: 'After full consideration of the action of the TUC in ordering a lightning strike in our industry we have come to the conclusion that our leaders acted unconstitutionally and against the terms of our agreement with the Master Printers' Association. We wish to make it clear that we retain our sympathy with the miners in their struggle for better wages, and working conditions, but we fail to see how ruin of other industries can bring this about.'

DAVIDSON. Wonderful. Can we make sure you emphasise *ruin*.

AMELIA *hesitates a moment*, REITH *nods*.

AMELIA. Of course.

The Home Secretary wishes to thank the people of London for their splendid response to his call for fifty thousand special constables. As upright as ever despite his eighty-five years, the Earl of Meath, originator of the Empire Day Movement, was sworn in as a special constable at Chertsey last night. Asked his age the Earl said: 'Eighty-five and still able to tackle a man. I box every morning.'

DAVIDSON. Is that true? Delightful.

REITH. Yes.

DAVIDSON. You should give him his own show.

AMELIA. Our programme tonight is as follows. Eight to nine-thirty: a variety programme including a topical strike sketch and a further episode of *That Child*. Ten to ten-thirty: some songs by Roy Henderson. Ten-thirty to twelve: dance music.

REITH. Wonderful, then let's get going, we've only five before transmission. Quite alright, Amelia?

AMELIA. Delightful.

DAVIDSON. The Home Secretary also will want to speak after the bulletin in the morning. He has an address for the nation. Nothing contentious. An appeal for volunteer constables. I said I was certain you wouldn't stand in his way.

REITH *nods*.

AMELIA. Of course.

AMELIA *exits. There's a silence*.

DAVIDSON. Thank you for listening.

REITH. Thank you for allowing me to disagree.

DAVIDSON. The Prime Minister has asked me to be clear –

REITH. Clarity is always gratefully received –

DAVIDSON. – that my role is not to cajole or control – it is to assess and aid you in your – difficult decisions about the appropriateness or otherwise about a particular item of news.

REITH. My role is to report the truth to those that listen.

Beat.

But I appreciate your help and advice.

Pause.

DAVIDSON. Commander Kenworthy was a good way out of line in the Commons, and you were even further out of line reporting on it.

REITH. Is that so?

DAVIDSON. You do understand, under emergency regulations we are quite within our powers to take over your organisation entirely?

REITH. And how might Commander Kenworthy react to that, does one think?

DAVIDSON. This crisis – it's sending us all mad, don't you think? But sanity will prevail.

DAVIDSON *exits*. REITH *is left. Ruminating*.

Scene Four

CHURCHILL *is laughing*.

CLEMMIE. I've brought you breakfast.

CHURCHILL. You've just missed a wonderful piece on the wireless, Jix shouting his appeal for special constables into next week.

CLEMMIE. Not a subtle man.

CHURCHILL. It was quite the thing – ALL RANKS OF THE / ARMED –

JIX (*a veritable shout*). ARMED FORCES OF THE CROWN ARE HEREBY INFORMED THAT ANY ACTION WHICH THEY MAY FIND NECESSARY TO TAKE IN AN HONEST ENDEAVOUR TO AID THE CIVIL POWER WILL RECEIVE, BOTH NOW AND AFTERWARDS, THE FULL SUPPORT OF HIS MAJESTY'S GOVERNMENT.

CHURCHILL. Wonderful. The man is so wonderfully – bellicose. He'd take on all-comers if he could. Just him wrapped in barbed wire, with a truncheon for a weapon. He'd flatten them all.

CLEMMIE. Shall I set it here?

CHURCHILL. Ah. Splendid.

CLEMMIE. Though how you don't just want to go back to sleep after eating it –

CHURCHILL. Be gentle with me, Clemmie. I've not had the best of it.

CLEMMIE. Have you not?

CHURCHILL. Tell me, how are you?

CLEMMIE. Winston, that is not a question you're interested in the answer to. How are you?

CHURCHILL. Dreadful.

CLEMMIE. You should simply not bother asking me anything, it'd make conversations flow more easily.

CHURCHILL. It has become quite the thing to attack me in the House.

CLEMMIE. I'm sure you face them bravely.

CHURCHILL. Meanwhile Baldwin walks on bloodless and unbloodied.

CLEMMIE. He's an accomplished politician.

CHURCHILL. And I am not one?

Pause. He looks at her, he chuckles.

You're quite right. I lack his ability to – I lack his ability to send others into war for him. I must always be first on the front. Meanwhile he drifts from place to place, dancing everything he wants into being without it even touching him. Do you know he visited the zoo yesterday? And went on a walk with his son. Where does he get his serenity?

CLEMMIE *kisses his forehead.*

CLEMMIE. Stay at the front. I like you there.

CHURCHILL. I thought my father was talking to me as I slept last night.

CLEMMIE. I'm sure even his ghost was pie-eyed.

CHURCHILL (*a laugh*). Quite right. Two drunk men caressing each other with conversation.

CLEMMIE. What did he say?

CHURCHILL. Nothing of importance, but how he *seemed* – that matters –

CLEMMIE. How did he seem?

CHURCHILL. Scared.

PETER. John. John…

REITH. Peter, now is not the time…

PETER. The Archbishop. He wants us to record his statement.

REITH. What statement?

PETER. A statement on behalf of all the churches to the people of the country… The Archbishop, on the BBC. John, this is a momentous day. You will broadcast it?

REITH. Of course I will – why wouldn't I?

BALDWIN. What does the statement say?

PETER *takes out a piece of paper.*

PETER. Representatives of the Christian churches in England are convinced that a real settlement will only be achieved in a spirit of fellowship and cooperation for the common good, and not as a result of war.

The stage lights up and the full cast is onstage, all reading it.

CHURCHILL. Realising that the longer the present struggle persists the greater will be the suffering and loss, they earnestly request that all the parties concerned in this dispute will agree to resume negotiations undeterred by obstacles which have been created by the events of the last few days.

REITH. If it should seem to be incumbent on us to suggest a definite line of approach, we would submit a return to the status quo of Friday last. Our proposal should be interpreted as involving simultaneously and concurrently –

CHURCHILL. He's writing policy now? The Church is writing policy?

BEVIN. Have you seen what's he done? Have you seen what he's written?

BALDWIN. One: The cancellation on the part of the TUC of the General Strike.

CHURCHILL. Sensible.

BALDWIN. Two: Renewal by the Government of its offer of assistance to the coal industry for a short definite period.

CHURCHILL. Less sensible.

BEVIN. The Archbishop of Canterbury, an unlikely ally.

PUGH. Jesus was a socialist.

BALDWIN. Three: The withdrawal on the part of the mine owners of the new wages scales recently issued.

BEVIN. Yes!

CHURCHILL. Outrageous and unchristian. Three points, and two of them are on their side.

DAVIDSON. The Archbishop wishes to broadcast it. What shall we do, sir?

PETER. Will you broadcast it? John?

DAVIDSON. Sir?

BALDWIN. Apologies. Thinking. Have you heard they derailed the *Flying Scotsman*? Managed to get it off the tracks. Cramlington. The BBC cannot broadcast this. The – Wuthering Heights must be stopped.

DAVIDSON. Understood, sir. May I recommend –

BALDWIN. But I mustn't be seen as censoring the Archbishop's words. The idea must come from the BBC itself, from Reith.

DAVIDSON. Prime Minister, John Reith is a firm Christian and I rather suspect…

BALDWIN. And the seeds of that idea – that censorship – cannot come from this office.

BALDWIN *thinks,* DAVIDSON *frowns, bewildered.*

Perhaps we might – suggest to an impassioned other that he might like to visit Savoy Hill – or wherever it is they hide that damn wireless – and contact Mr Reith directly. Perhaps his passion might be of some use to us here.

There's a pause, and then DAVIDSON *smiles.*

DAVIDSON. That's – um – I rather think that might be brilliant.

BALDWIN. Your Prime Minister is occasionally capable of it.

A phone rings. CHURCHILL *picks it up.*

CHURCHILL. Winston. How can I help?

Scene Five

BILLY BENNETT.
    I'm cherishing a secret in my bosom
    About this dreadful stage-life that I lead
    I've heard it said that Pro's are decent people
    But according to the papers that I read
    Both actresses and actors are dead 'wrong-uns'
    Whether from the 'Palace' or the 'Hippodrome'
    The chaps I meet outside know I'm an actor
    But I never breathe a word of it at home.
    So, my mother doesn't know I'm on the stage
    It would break her poor old heart if she found out
    She knows I'm a deserter,
    From the Scottish Fusiliers
    She knows I stole a blind-man's can,
    That got me seven years!
    She knows I've been connected
    With a gang of West-End Pests
    And the police have had me twice inside the cage
    And she knows I mix with ladies that have got a shady past
    But my mother doesn't know I'm on the stage.
    Sometimes she sees the powder on my clothing
    And then it's such a nuisance to explain
    If she thought that it was powder she'd go crazy
    Of course, I have to tell her it's cocaine.

CHURCHILL. I've been listening to your wireless.

    REITH *turns off the radio. He stands up.*

REITH. Have you?

CHURCHILL. Become rather a fan of Uncle Caractacus. And Aunt Phyllis.

REITH. You listened to *Children's Hour*?

CHURCHILL. Wanted to know the children you're making. I found the nightingale's song quite enchanting. Perhaps a little more attention to practical schoolwork might help. Arithmetic seemed lacking. But I did – enjoy it.

REITH. We'll take your views into account. About the arithmetic.

CHURCHILL. I also – this must be a few days ago – enjoyed your news piece on the – schoolchildren – children of strikers – running their own lessons. Uplifting. Extraordinary what people are capable of. An American friend of mine, wonderful chap, news man like you…

REITH *walks over to a cabinet. He gets a whisky for* CHURCHILL.

REITH. I am not a news man. I am a broadcaster.

CHURCHILL. Ah, whisky, wonderful. Over here on business, says he's never seen anything like this…

REITH. None of us have.

CHURCHILL. Bicycles, he's amazed by the bicycles, saw one man on a what he was certain was a penny-farthing. Not sure I believe that.

REITH. No.

CHURCHILL. But what has most impressed him, is the fortitude of the British people – if someone steps on another person's toes – even if they are furious with them – they are still quick to say – 'I beg your pardon.' It is the spirit – the spirit of our people that will see us through.

REITH. Then why do you worry about the Communists at all?

CHURCHILL. An about-turn, I'm impressed.

REITH. I'm not trying to impress you.

CHURCHILL. Taking me with the castle, when I was staring at your queen. Close to a hundred thousand pounds, they've invested. The Soviets. Solely in the Communist Party of this country. Solely for the purpose of fermenting discord. They even ran a candidate against me in the last election, did you know that?

REITH. I did not.

CHURCHILL. Everyone always thinks we should be afraid of enemies we can't see – well, I tell you the enemies I'm most afraid of are those that stand in front of you and shout in your face 'I am your enemy'. And these Soviets…

REITH. Yes.

CHURCHILL. Have you read Marx? It's fascinating. They're not just hopeful of revolution in this country, they're dependent upon it. Russia is an over-agriculturalised nightmare, they need forward-thinking industry, they need our mines, our steelworks, our industrialised workforce. It's all in there. They need big industry. They need us. Or Germany. Or both.

REITH. If you're here to tell me I can't broadcast the Archbishop then…

CHURCHILL. For the record, I wish it noted, that it was you who brought the Archbishop into this conversation, not I…

REITH. Is it not the case?

CHURCHILL. I believe in a free press. I believe in it operating without great interference. I have spent my life and will spend the rest of it fighting against tyranny. But if you were to ask me which was more important, free press or a free country, I'd only have one reply. We are drowning, sir, these strikers they're not just denying us their work, they're denying other people from working at all. They're inching us towards either ruin or revolution. We need life support. Will you provide it?

REITH. I feel I am.

CHURCHILL. The Archbishop's voice is a welcome one, but he is misguided.

REITH. Finally. Thank you. And what would you wish me do? Censor the most powerful man in our Church?

Pause. CHURCHILL *studies* REITH's *face.*

CHURCHILL. Imagine a scenario. Am I right – I believe I am – in saying the BBC contract expires at the end of this year?

REITH *looks up, his fear palpable.*

REITH. I was assured it was a formality, the BBC becomes a corporation, no longer a company but supported, the royal charter, empowered for the nation by our licence fee to –

CHURCHILL. Imagine – I've travelled to America – they're awfully innovative about how they're funding their programmes – they advertise – there was a jingle about soap that became an earworm for me. Imagine there are suddenly – perhaps – competitors for your bandwidth. Imagine you're free, no need for a licence fee, for the advertisers will support you.

REITH. Advertising does not – There would be no *Children's Hour* – for who can advertise sink cleaner during it –

CHURCHILL. These advertisers are frightfully clever and remarkably entertaining, I'm sure you'd innovate and –

REITH. Mr Churchill, radio should entertain, but it is not for entertainment alone, it must also inform and educate. Advertisement radio may think it gives the public what it wants, but it simply creates a fictitious demand for lower standards. The BBC allows us to protect what is important. The sabbath, the educational components of our – the Shakespeare I am making available to all –

CHURCHILL. You have thought it through wonderfully clearly, I can see. I was just – positing the suggestion. It would be a hideous future I'm sure.

Pause.

REITH. But you threaten it nonetheless?

CHURCHILL. Young man, the only threats in this room are to me. Your supposed news broadcast about me was petulant, don't think I didn't listen, and I am aware that by being here I risk more petulance, and yet I come all the same – why? Because I believe in my cause.

Pause.

You know my father was briefly leader of the Commons – and Chancellor of the Exchequer.

REITH. I do.

CHURCHILL. He was the politician most likely. When he spoke – everyone listened. His words were tremendously powerful.

REITH. You've inherited some of his skills.

CHURCHILL. He was twice the man I am or ever can be. He resigned because he thought he could engineer a coup – he thought he could become Prime Minister and he knew that he needed that – to not just be significant – but be the most significant…

REITH. A tragedy some men labour under.

CHURCHILL. We all have our roles. And we are all played within them.

REITH. This isn't my fiefdom, I believe in what we the BBC can be, the role of the BBC.

CHURCHILL. And I believe in the Conservative Government and the Archbishop believes in his Church, and these union men, they believe in their union. Competing significances, every one. So the question becomes – what will we trade to others in order to keep our own organisation's significance? Government – it is such a trade – a constant battle – those I have to face in the Commons – those I have to face without – but I have my lines, beyond which I won't compromise and you must have them too. Is the Archbishop such a line, I wonder?

REITH. I am a Christian.

CHURCHILL. All the best people are. My point is, my father's lines overwhelmed him, he could see nothing but lines. I am his junior in every respect except that of having learnt compromise. In order to pursue my advancement and, crucially, the advancement of my most significant beliefs.

REITH. Mr Churchill, please do not put me in this situation –

CHURCHILL. I have not. It is the circumstances of the times that have put you in this situation. You hold the future like a precious glass globe, I merely advise you on what you might do with that future.

REITH *says nothing. His brain churning with possibilities.*

The only thing I would say. Advise. If you were to – if you perhaps could see the matter from the Government's side – and were to disappoint the Archbishop – for all our futures – not least that of the BBC – the Government would prefer it that this message came from you personally rather than – us. Can't be seen to be interfering in the affairs of the cloth.

Beat.

The glass globe waits, Mr Reith.

Scene Six

HELGA. Abide with me, fast falls the eventide
The darkness deepens Lord, with me abide
Whcn other helpers fail and comforts flee
Help of the helpless, oh, abide with me.

REITH *gets to his knees and begins to pray.*

Swift to its close ebbs out life's little day
Earth's joys grow dim, its glories pass away
Change and decay in all around I see
O Thou who changest not, abide with me

MURIEL. What a beautiful voice.

REITH. Yes, I rather like it too.

He turns off the radio.

MURIEL. I'm interrupting you praying.

REITH. Merely seeking answers.

MURIEL. Answers to what?

REITH. I'm unsure. How can I help?

MURIEL. I brought you four cheese sandwiches and a Chelsea bun. I presumed you would be here tonight.

REITH. Why would you presume that?

MURIEL. It may seem funny to say – but I could hear it in your tone as you delivered the news.

REITH. Am I so transparent?

MURIEL. Most pray for sustenance and charity. But you – you exclusively pray for guidance – for your answers. Quite admirable really.

REITH. Arrogant, I'm sure. He has larger matters to attend to than me.

MURIEL. He has larger matters to attend to than my needs too. Perhaps you might find answers closer at hand.

Pause.

REITH. It has been made clear to me that the BBC is – that I am – that all this is rather more vulnerable than I thought. Unless, that is, I was – I could – I do – show more diligence to the Government line.

MURIEL. Is that diligence hard to follow?

REITH. Don't look so frustrated with me.

MURIEL. Some might say – in my position – it is just the wireless, John.

REITH. Some might reply – it is not *just* anything.

MURIEL. Tell me then – what does the BBC do now that it wouldn't do under Government control? They'd allow your ridiculous orchestras –

REITH. What is ridiculous about an orchestra?

MURIEL. They'd allow your so-called comedy.

REITH. You're being obnoxious, Muriel.

MURIEL. What wouldn't they allow?

REITH. The truth.

MURIEL. Are you telling the truth now?

Pause.

REITH. I wish you wouldn't come in such a state – cheese sandwiches have little worth if you distract me – I hate it when you're disappointed –

MURIEL. Because you care how I feel or because you care how it makes you feel?

REITH. Twisting, always twisting –

MURIEL (*her fury beginning to swell*). What did you ever care for the truth?

REITH. Careful.

MURIEL. Maybe this company is as dishonest as you are.

REITH. Muriel, please.

MURIEL. Hiding in plain sight, your deviousness concealed behind a face that never tremors.

REITH. I am not devious.

MURIEL. You always hid from it. How you felt. How others did.

REITH. Careful, Muriel.

MURIEL. The man who married the woman that the other man loved. The man who loved the man who loved the woman that he himself married. The man who tangled himself in knots.

REITH. You don't understand –

MURIEL. Do you deny you married me because the man you
loved happened to love me?

REITH. Yes, of course I deny it. That is simply not the case.

MURIEL. You loved him, he loved me, and you decided to
square the circle in the queerest possible way by making me
believe… That's truth. Do you see it, John? Do you? If you
can't – then truth matters not a damn to you and you're
fighting – you're hurting yourself – for nothing much at all.

She exits.

Scene Seven

REITH *walks forward, and as he does the world transforms
around him. We feel the weight of his strides, we feel the pain
around him.*

BEVIN. We are not declaring war on the people. War has been
declared by the Government pushed on by sordid capitalism.
The best brains of this movement are available to help find
a solution for this country of this great problem.

CHURCHILL. In order to pursue my advancement and,
crucially, the advancement of my most significant beliefs.

CHARLIE. They, looking back, all the eastern side beheld
Of Paradise, so late their happy seat,
Waved over by that flaming brand, the gate
With dreadful faces thronged and fiery arms:
Some natural tears they dropped, but wiped them soon;
The world was all before them, where to choose
Their place of rest, and Providence their guide;
They, hand in hand, with wandering steps and slow,
Through Eden took their solitary way.

MURIEL. 'Be strong and of good courage, fear not, nor be afraid of them; for the Lord thy God, he it is that doth go with thee; he will not fail thee, nor forsake thee.' Deuteronomy, 31:6.

REITH. Your Grace. John Reith. I was told I'd find you here.

ARCHBISHOP. And how can I help you, Mr Reith?

REITH. John Reith, Your Grace, from the BBC.

ARCHBISHOP. Ah, yes, I recognise the name now. Sorry, when you get to my age, you find your memory becomes fleeting. Luckily, my faith has held strong. I don't have a wireless, Mr Reith, but many of my parishioners do, and a good portion of my clergy, I know it's proved a great help to some of them.

REITH. We've tried to behave as a Christian company should, sir.

ARCHBISHOP. The country is lucky to have you.

REITH. The country is lucky to have you, Your Grace. I was here last Easter for your sermon on abstinence in a time of Lent. It was very powerful.

ARCHBISHOP. Lent is an easy subject to preach upon. Everyone likes the idea of doing without. Denial is, in many ways, the easiest form of worship. Or that's what I've always thought.

Pause.

You're here about arrangements for my speech?

REITH. No. I'm here to tell you that unfortunately we won't be able to broadcast it.

The disappointment echoes.

ARCHBISHOP. Ah.

REITH. We are in a position of considerable delicacy…

ARCHBISHOP. The whole country is.

REITH. A simpler statement I could broadcast – making clear
that – you have sympathy but that you – The trouble is
you're so specific, Your Grace, with the answers. And for
a government that is trying to navigate its way through the
crisis – your interventions are –

ARCHBISHOP. Problematic.

REITH. Yes, sir.

ARCHBISHOP. The Government don't want my piece to be
broadcast.

REITH. I did not say that –

ARCHBISHOP. No. You did not.

REITH. I would have you speak on any subject. I'd broadcast
your sermons to the world. And yet this –

ARCHBISHOP. I was compelled to write it. It's something
I prayed on and I came to the realisation that there are those
out there that are begging for us to help them – to find
a solution that doesn't leave them wretched and that we, as
a modern society, as a Christian society, have an obligation
to listen. I've tried to – take some walks – pay some visits –
and the suffering I see…

REITH. I see it too.

ARCHBISHOP. I'm not sure you do. I'm not sure this would be
the position you'd take if you had. But blindness is a preserve
of the privileged, I suppose.

REITH *says nothing. The* ARCHBISHOP *looks at him.*

You're absolutely sure? You cannot broadcast?

REITH. If we do so… We have not been commandeered but
there have been strong representations to the effect that this
should be done. If we – do not support a governmental line.

ARCHBISHOP. Some honesty. You are frightened?

REITH. Our independence matters…

ARCHBISHOP. But following one's own conscience is independence.

REITH. And there might be future consequences – our future position may be fatally compromised. And how would we protect the sabbath? From jazz and variety.

Pause.

ARCHBISHOP. I am not political. I present no threat to the Government of this country. If I were to make representations to them…

REITH. This is my – doing. I am the only one you can make representations to Your Grace.

ARCHBISHOP. And this decision is final?

REITH. It has to be. I am truly – humbly – sorry.

ARCHBISHOP. I bear you no ill will.

REITH. Thank you. Thank you.

ARCHBISHOP. I will pray for you, John Reith.

Pause. He looks up at the ARCHBISHOP.

REITH. May I ask – may I ask – if it's not too much to ask – may we pray together, Your Grace?

ARCHBISHOP. Of course we can.

They both kneel.

Almighty God, unto whom all hearts are open,
all desires known, and from whom no secrets are hid –

REITH *lets out a series of small sharp breaths.*

Are you quite well, my son?

REITH. Yes.

ARCHBISHOP. Then why might you not seem it?

REITH. I am – beset by – uh – demons. And – I don't know if they're of my own making.

ARCHBISHOP. If the path of goodness was easy then everyone would walk down it.

REITH. I loved another – I love another –

ARCHBISHOP. Than your wife? Open your heart to her and you will find that love again.

REITH. I married her for the wrong – I married her – wrong –

ARCHBISHOP. Then find the right reasons for staying married to her.

REITH. I can't find the right reasons for anything. Or I can and then – they float away – I lie, I cheat, I try to be –

ARCHBISHOP (*harder*). Then those are sins and they need addressing.

REITH. I think – I think what I'm doing – it matters – and –

ARCHBISHOP. Nothing of what we do allows us to be anything other than good. There is no job so great that it disallows morality.

REITH. But if what it achieves is in the greater good then maybe –

ARCHBISHOP. There is no greater good, there is simply good. Great has no place beside goodness.

Pause.

I cannot absolve you of your choices, Mr Reith, I cannot even make your choices for you, there are many paths that I can help you see, but the journey is yours and yours alone.

REITH. I feel like shouting to God, oh God, where is my certainty –

ARCHBISHOP. God would tell you, it is there. Inside. You must listen for it, and when you hear it, you must act on it. That is your obligation as his follower. That is your obligation as a human whomsoever is your god. It is only you who can decide what you are, and what you want your life to be, and what you want your BBC to be. You are a leader, Mr Reith, because you chose to be one – just as I did. And now you must lead yourself.

Beat. These words have an effect all can see.

Does all this alter how you feel about the question of whether I should be broadcast?

Beat. REITH *thinks, and thinks and thinks again.*

REITH. No.

ARCHBISHOP. Then you have found one certainty at least. Are you ready for prayer?

Beat.

REITH. Yes

ARCHBISHOP. Almighty God, unto whom all hearts are open, all desires known, and from whom no secrets are hid; Cleanse the thoughts of our hearts by the inspiration of thy Holy Spirit, that we may perfectly love thee, and worthily magnify thy holy Name; through Christ our Lord.

Amen.

REITH. Amen.

Scene Eight

BEVIN *and* PUGH *approach the* ENGINEER.

BEVIN. Good morning, we're here to see Mr Reith.

ENGINEER. That's not going to happen.

PUGH. We demand to see him.

ENGINEER. Demanding now, is it?

BEVIN. The British Broadcasting Company. British. For Britain. Does he understand what that means?

ENGINEER. For the nation, sir, and that is something we take very seriously.

BEVIN. I understand not giving us time at his microphones but to deny the Archbishop…

ENGINEER. I wouldn't know about that. Beyond my domain.

BEVIN. Does he know what he's cost us? They need to hear the noise we're making.

ENGINEER. Mr Reith has an important organisation to run. I believe you both do too, dear. So why don't you hurry along and run it?

BEVIN. May you give him a message? May you tell him I understand what he protects. As a child I would read the paper aloud to my family because they were illiterate. Tell him workers need his wireless.

He shuts the door. The unionists walk away, dejected, just as CHURCHILL *arrives triumphant – he approaches* BALDWIN.

CHURCHILL. Nearly four thousand trains will run today.

BALDWIN. Any new fatalities to report?

CHURCHILL. Prime Minister, that is not an upbeat response…

BALDWIN. My uncle was on a train through the west of England yesterday, due to disembark at Bristol instead it sailed right through, the volunteer piloting the vehicle couldn't get it to stop. There were also three fatalities in Edinburgh when a goods train ploughed into the back of a passenger train. I could go on…

CHURCHILL. Have you noticed? We're winning, Stanley.

BALDWIN. The posts have not been passed.

CHURCHILL. But they are in sight.

BALDWIN *looks at him, irritated. Then he calms his face.*

BALDWIN. Yes, and I should thank you, Winston.

CHURCHILL. I did everything I could in the service of my government –

BALDWIN. And you have served it – admirably. Without damage to *my* government's reputation at all. The spectre to haunt people with and keep them in line – not least, well I suppose, in particular the BBC –

CHURCHILL *is surprised*.

CHURCHILL. You think I've haunted them for you?

BALDWIN. Oh, no, you did it because you disliked Wuthering Heights more than you disliked me. Thank you, Winston.

CHURCHILL *turns and looks at him. And a House of Commons partially rises around us.*

SPEAKER. The Right Honourable Gentleman for Carnarvon Boroughs.

There's cheering.

LLOYD GEORGE. I would ask the Chancellor of the Exchequer why the Archbishop of Canterbury's very important letter on behalf of the churches of this country was not published in the Government '*Gazette*' and why it was suppressed in its broadcasting on the vital BBC.

CHURCHILL *sways slightly.*

SPEAKER. The Chancellor of the Exchequer.

There's a roar from the chamber. Mainly of derision.
CHURCHILL looks around – surprised by his unpopularity.

CHURCHILL. The *Gazette* had no space. But as for broadcasting. I cannot answer any question for which I have not even a general responsibility.

MEMBERS. Who is responsible?

CHURCHILL. Instead, that question must be addressed to the proper department.

MEMBERS. Which department?

SPEAKER. The Member for Caerphilly.

MORGAN JONES. Like the Right Honourable Gentleman for Carnarvon Boroughs I want to ask in relation to the matter of the Archbishop being denied a platform, and wish to know to whom we are to address questions regarding broadcasting in this House. Perhaps the Prime Minister may be able to assist me if no one else can?

MEMBERS. Hear hear.

SPEAKER. The Prime Minister.

There's more cheering.

BALDWIN. I agree with our Chancellor that he has no such formal responsibility, but as his knowledge is greater than mine, and as he's done such sterling work as we all know during this strike, perhaps he might provide the House with some limited guidance…

He's throwing him under a bus, the members ooh.

CHURCHILL *looks at him, astonished, as he rises.*

SPEAKER. The Chancellor of the Exchequer.

There are further cries of derision.

CHURCHILL. Thank you, Prime Minister. (*He thinks.*) During this crisis our people were starved of information by the actions of the strikers, the newspapers were suppressed by their work and their work alone. The *Gazette* was used to give the country information regarding what is proceeding in all parts, and also to sustain the nation in the difficult period through which we are passing.

He looks at BALDWIN, *who has a strange smile on his face.*

As far as broadcasting, I state again, my knowledge of the matter is limited…

There are howls of derision.

…but I did – as the Prime Minister so generously states, have some oversight – and can tell you the decision to not broadcast His Grace, the Archbishop of Canterbury, came from the BBC and the BBC alone.

Scene Nine

REITH *is lying across the front of the stage*. CHARLIE *approaches, brimming with anger.*

CHARLIE. What have you done?

REITH. Charlie, don't –

CHARLIE. Muriel, you ask Muriel… you propose to Muriel…

REITH. We can love her together, we'll find a way.

CHARLIE. I found her… for me…

REITH. I know, but it hasn't worked out that way.

CHARLIE. Because of you.

REITH. Don't be angry, she'll still be in your life.

CHARLIE. You told me you didn't even want marriage.

REITH. You convinced me otherwise.

CHARLIE. And so you decide to not only marry before me but marry the one I thought I might choose.

REITH. Ask her too. Make it her choice.

CHARLIE. I have no interest in competing with you, Johnnie.

REITH. No.

CHARLIE. Call this off.

REITH. I can't. I've phoned my mother. There are things in progress…

CHARLIE. Do this and you cut me open. Cut me open and I might not be able to see you again.

REITH. Of course you can see me. This way you can see us both – we could all – live together, I was thinking – perhaps then –

CHARLIE *kisses* REITH *hungrily. And then breaks off.*

REITH *stands, swaying under the weight of it.*

CHARLIE. Do you even like her?

REITH. Of course I do.

CHARLIE. And love?

REITH. I think we will make a good pair. And with you – with you – we can build a life –

CHARLIE. The fairy stories you tell yourself. About what is possible and what is not.

REITH. You like her, you like me.

CHARLIE. Don't you see what you've done – don't you see –

REITH. You did it first.

CHARLIE. You'll crumple without me.

REITH. I crumple with you! You broke what we had –

CHARLIE. So this is revenge?

REITH. I am doing what is necessary in order to keep whatever life I have. This way –

CHARLIE. There is no this way, there is only your way and it is perverted – and I will have nothing to do with it.

CHARLIE *makes to walk away.* REITH *grabs at him.* CHARLIE *pushes him back.* REITH *lands hard on the floor and stays there.*

Always so hysterical.

REITH. Isn't that what love is? Hysteria?

CHARLIE. You have done the wrong thing in the wrong way.

REITH. This is all I can do – this is all I can – YOU DID THIS FIRST. YOU DID THIS FIRST.

ISABEL. Mr Reith? Mr Reith? John.

CHARLIE *is gone.* REITH *looks around for him.*

REITH. Yes.

ISABEL. I heard shouting.

REITH. Oh. I heard – nothing.

ISABEL. I've made you tea, sir, and found you a nice biscuit.

REITH. Yes.

ISABEL. I was rather hoping they might encourage you to get off the floor.

REITH. No.

ISABEL. Perhaps I could join you – on the floor –

REITH. No.

ISABEL. Lie beside you, encourage you to rise up.

REITH. Do you love the BBC, Isabel?

ISABEL. Yes. I do in fact.

REITH. You know, it's the strangest thing, I hadn't a clue what broadcasting was when I took this job and now I can't imagine life without it.

ISABEL. My husband gets so irritated – must we have this beastly thing on all the time – but I have to listen.

REITH. Why?

ISABEL. For the – possibilities of it. The joke I never anticipated, the music that transports me from my washing-up to a concert hall, for the pleasure of listening to the passion of others – not just reading their words but hearing it in their voice. When I hear something of a lesser standard I am not just disappointed, I'm angry that they'd treat our wireless so. Have I said too much?

REITH. No.

ISABEL. Wind her up and watch her go my husband always says.

REITH. Your husband doesn't sound –

ISABEL. No, he isn't, but if I turn the set up loud enough it drowns him out.

REITH *laughs*.

Why do you love it, sir?

REITH *thinks*.

REITH. Because it lays us bare. You can lie in print. You can
make yourself another. But on the wireless – someone will –
not everyone – but someone will hear it in you. The tiny catch
in your voice not even you can prevent. The way your words
sound. A microphone opens you out, makes you honest.

Pause. ISABEL *smiles.*

Are you smiling?

ISABEL. Yes, sir. I've always thought the same, sir. It hides
nothing.

REITH. What would you do? With my job?

ISABEL. I'd like more stories from the war. We seem to be all
trying to forget it. But whether it's the fact that nine per cent
of all British men under the age of forty-five have died,
making singledom more than a possibility for some of us, or
that women were able to be policemen for the first time, or
the Women's Army Auxiliary Corps and the battle for that…

REITH. Sounds quite like one for *Women's Hour*.

ISABEL. With all due respect, sir, it's not, that's just my
perspective, it should be a show, a series of shows about all
our experiences of the war. The damage done, the scars left.
Male and female.

REITH. You weren't in the police, were you?

ISABEL. I was, as it happens. And then I served in France.
I needed to do my bit.

REITH. The secrets we hide. That sounds like a good
programme. Any other thoughts?

ISABEL. More comedy. And possibly less – talking about
music – I never really understand discussion of music – play
the music – don't bally talk about it.

REITH *smiles. He looks across at* ISABEL.

REITH. Are you religious, Isabel?

ISABEL. You know I am, sir, it was the first question you asked when you interviewed me.

REITH. Yes. Yes. Well, today, I denied the Archbishop of Canterbury airtime he wants and needs –

ISABEL. Oh. That seems a shame.

REITH. In four hours he'll make a statement in front of Canterbury Cathedral. And we will not be there to capture it.

ISABEL. Why?

REITH. Because I believe…

Pause.

Because I believe in the BBC. In what it can be. And I believe it must be – and I believe that's more important than – I believe its survival is more important than my – salvation.

Pause.

Soldiers with bayonets fixed charged into strikers in Hull today. Have you heard?

ISABEL. No.

REITH. No. Well, we won't report it. No bayonets. No archbishops. Many returning to work – strike breaking – all over in fact – we shall report that.

Pause.

Two questions. First question: may we talk again about your servicemen idea?

ISABEL. Servicemen and women, sir.

REITH. Yes.

ISABEL. I'd like that, sir.

REITH. Second question: what biscuit is it you brought?

ISABEL. A ginger nut, sir.

REITH. Aha.

ISABEL. I thought you might say that.

Scene Ten

Back in the studio.

ENGINEER. And how many spoons do you intend on playing?

BRUCE. Just bought the forty with me.

ENGINEER. You want to play forty spoons?

BRUCE. I *have* to play forty spoons. This what I'm playing in to?

ENGINEER. That's the microphone, yes.

BRUCE. Can you get it lower?

ENGINEER. No.

BRUCE. It's just I can't get my knee up that high.

ENGINEER. I can see.

BRUCE. For the spoons.

ENGINEER. The forty spoons.

BRUCE. Yes.

ENGINEER. Why do you need forty, dear?

BRUCE. Why do you need the microphone so high up, you
    beggar?

    REITH *enters on the charge.* AMELIA *and* PETER *trailing
    after him.*

AMELIA. But I have the words…

REITH. I understand that, Amelia, but…

PETER. Let him do it.

AMELIA. Yes, sir.

ENGINEER. Sir?

PETER. We need the room.

ENGINEER. They've settled?

BRUCE. Who? Oh cripes.

Suddenly BALDWIN, PUGH *and* BEVIN *are in the room too.*

PUGH. As a result of the possibilities we see in getting back to negotiations, we are here today, sir, to say that this General Strike is to be terminated forthwith. That is the announcement which my general council is empowered to make.

He wipes his forehead, he looks at BEVIN, *who nods.*

BALDWIN *smiles.*

BALDWIN. All I would say in answer to that is I thank God for your decision.

BEVIN. In return and in the spirit of our compromise – we would like you to give us an idea of whether there is to be a resumption of mining operations or whether all the negotiations have to be carried on while the miners still remain out.

BALDWIN. My object, of course, is to get the mines started at the first moment possible and get an agreement reached. I cannot say any more at this meeting now.

BEVIN. So we can have no word?

BALDWIN. Mr Pugh, Mr Bevin, all three of us have got a great deal to do, and the sooner you get to your work and I get to mine –

PUGH. So you're giving us nothing?

BALDWIN. I wouldn't say nothing.

BEVIN. Can we at least meet soon?

BALDWIN. I have a country to run, Mr Bevin, and you have your – important work. I think it may be that whatever decision I come to as regards the mines, the House of Commons may be the best place in which to declare it. Await that. My speech there.

BEVIN. But, sir – I just think…

BALDWIN (*harder*). The time for your thinking has passed –
wouldn't you say? Now is the time for doing and setting
right.

BEVIN. We couldn't keep everyone together – if they could
have only heard the noise we were – making…

BALDWIN. Well, they did not. Or if they did, they found the
noise to be either not one they liked or inconsequential.
Thank you, Mr Pugh. Mr Bevin.

BRUCE. The TUC have settled? On what terms?

AMELIA. I don't think there are terms. Word is they've just –
given up.

A phone rings from off. They all turn towards it. PETER
signals to the ENGINEER *to get it.*

ENGINEER. Right you are.

REITH. Thank you, Peter – thank you for your service through
this – it's been most – You've done a good job.

PETER. Have I?

REITH. And you too of course, Amelia. Strong work.

AMELIA. Thank you, sir. Wonderful to get through it, sir. Can't
wait to get a normal bally bus again.

ENGINEER. It's the Prime Minister, sir, on the telephone…

BALDWIN. Mr Reith…

REITH. Prime Minister.

PETER *looks at* REITH *– who nods. He picks up another
phone.*

BALDWIN. I wanted to express my thanks for the great help
and service the BBC provided through this.

REITH. Thank you, Prime Minister.

BALDWIN. The restrictions placed upon the press threw
a heavy burden of responsibility on you, but the way you

discharged your task, in the face of exceptional difficulties, deserves the greatest of credit upon yourself and all who helped you in the work.

REITH. Thank you, sir.

BALDWIN. Well, I won't keep you, I know you're probably standing by to deliver the news.

REITH. Yes, sir.

BALDWIN. They've sent you the statement to read?

REITH. Yes, sir.

BALDWIN. Good. Good. Well, warm appreciation to you. I think you made all the difference.

REITH puts down the phone. There's a heaviness to him. PETER puts his phone down too.

REITH. How long do I have?

ENGINEER. Ninety seconds, sir.

He sits and looks at the microphone.

REITH. Perhaps all those that aren't necessary for the broadcast could leave.

PETER. Including me?

REITH. Yes. And who's this man...

BRUCE. I'm due to be playing spoons. Bought my best set.

REITH. We won't be needing your services today. Amelia, will you escort him out?

AMELIA. Of course.

She gestures for him to leave.

BRUCE. But... but... my old mum's listening.

REITH. She'll want to be listening anyway.

BRUCE. I can't believe they've settled. That's us done, don't they know that?

They exit. PETER *lingers a moment more.*

REITH. You know, Peter, I think we've done a great thing here.

PETER. Are you sure?

REITH. Consider this: If there'd been broadcasting during the French Revolution – it's more than possible there wouldn't have been a French Revolution. All that bloodshed – spared, isn't that worth the – worth it…

PETER. Perhaps.

REITH *looks at* PETER *desperately.*

REITH. You do understand, it would – I would – it would have been better for me to fight as you would have had us fight. I am a religious man, I denied the Archbishop a voice. But for the BBC – we've just secured the future of this great institution –

PETER. The trouble is, I'm also thinking of all the good we could have done. The possibilities of all this – of the BBC – which I built – when others couldn't and wouldn't – was to make something better. Instead, we made all the difference. And secured our future.

He exits. REITH *waits for the countdown, so do we. The* ENGINEER *signals him in.*

REITH. This is London and all stations calling…

He pauses.

At a meeting with the Prime Minister at 10, Downing Street, Mr Pugh announced on behalf of the TUC that the General Strike is terminating today. He released the following statement:

'In order to resume negotiations, the TUC has decided to end the General Strike today and instructions are being sent to the general secretaries of all affiliated unions. Members before acting must await the definite instructions from their executive councils.'

The Prime Minister further commented:

'The General Strike is over, though several days will elapse before normality is restored. It has ended without conditions entered into by the Government. Our business is not to triumph over those who have failed in a mistaken attempt. It is rather to rally together the population as a whole in an attempt to restore the well-being of the nation.'

CHURCHILL *opens a bottle of champagne, as he does so the* FOLEY ARTISTS *fire a gun. He looks at it spill across the floor.*

CHURCHILL. Clemmie? Clemmie. We've done it. We beat them.

REITH. Our first feeling on hearing of the termination of the General Strike must be one of profound thankfulness to Almighty God, who has led us through this supreme trial with national health unimpaired. Our second is to those here on earth who have aided the struggle.

ISABEL. One-point-seven million workers downed tools as one on the 3rd May 1926. Mostly they did so not for their own benefit, for no improvement in their own conditions, but as a unified action to protect the downtrodden miners. It was – and remains – the only General Strike in Britain's history.

The Archbishop's speech was read in full by Amelia Johnson on the one p.m. bulletin on the 11th May. But it was three days late and by that time it had no teeth to it, for history had moved on. On the 12th May the TUC declared the strike at an end. But as the transport workers, printers and those involved in electricity and gas returned to their jobs, the miners – stayed out. They would until December, when extreme cold and hunger forced them back to work. Needless to say neither the General Strike nor their subsequent persistence resulted in any sort of victory – less money and longer hours were conceded.

The BBC was made a corporation at the end of 1926 – cementing its position at the heart of the British establishment – and John Reith swiftly became a sir. Even when he left the BBC, he tried as hard as he could to retain the BBC's monopoly position on broadcasting believing it necessary for the good of the people. In 1954 the British Government decided to increase competition and commercial television was born with ITV. The Prime Minister of that government? Winston Churchill.

REITH. Yes, all that's left for me to say is…

All for me left to say is…

In going to work tomorrow or the next day, could we not all go as fellow craftsmen, united in a determination to pick up the broken pieces, to repair the gaps and build up the walls of a more enduring city – the city revealed to the mystic eyes of William Blake…

And did those feet in Ancient Times
Walk upon England's mountains green
And was the holy Lamb of God,
On England's pleasant pastures seen!

CHURCHILL. Clemmie. Clemmie. He's reading Blake. The poor bastard is reading Blake.

REITH. And did the Countenance Divine,
Shine forth upon our clouded hills?
And was Jerusalem builded here,
Among these dark Satanic Mills?

REITH *and* CHURCHILL. Bring me my Bow of burning gold;
Bring me my Arrows of desire:
Bring me my Spear: O clouds unfold!
Bring me my Chariot of fire!

I will not cease from Mental Fight,
Nor shall my Sword sleep in my hand:
Till we have built Jerusalem,
In England's green & pleasant Land.

There's a pause.

The two men stand looking out. Like both of them have lost something.

CHURCHILL. We beat them, Clemmie. Showed the red mist the door. And yet –

CLEMMIE. I know.

CHURCHILL. I fear this was my chance.

CLEMMIE. There'll be another.

CHURCHILL. That bastard Baldwin –

CLEMMIE. I know.

CHURCHILL. He doesn't understand leadership. He doesn't understand what I do for him. Or rather he does and plays me admirably.

REITH. This is London, and now to – Well, this is wonderful, one of my favourite programmes, and now to Marion Cran and her *Gardener's Chat*.

MARION. Thank you, Mr Reith, today on our show we're going to be discussing how to look after those pesky Aspidistras and whether indeed they're worth the effort, and then we'll be playing a topical talk from Mr H. Thorogood on 'The Glory of Tulips'…

REITH *turns off the radio.*

He is shaking.

ENGINEER. That's us then, sir.

REITH. Yes.

ENGINEER. Can I fetch you – ?

REITH. No. I'm perfectly fine. Just a moment's peace – please.

ENGINEER. Of course, sir. Enjoyed the Blake, sir. Very rousing.

REITH. Was it rousing?

ENGINEER. Very, sir. I wanted to sing along.

REITH *looks up.*

REITH. I didn't – sing – did I?

ENGINEER. No, sir. Very good, sir.

REITH. People didn't hear me sing?

ENGINEER. No, sir.

REITH. Thank you.

The ENGINEER *exits.*

REITH *stands. He walks around the room.*

Charlie?

He listens. No noise comes.

Charlie?

But no ghosts come.

Oh.

He is entirely overcome. He hears a thousand noises in his head.

Then he straightens. He looks out.

Blackout.